WE LOVE TO COOK. YOU LOVE TO EAT. WE LOVE TO

Meatballs
FOR THE PEOPLE

Mathias Pilblad

Life is all about family and meatballs.
I love you Linda, Jack and Viggo.

Meatballs

FOR THE PEOPLE

**Recipes from the cult
Stockholm restaurant**

Mathias Pilblad

BLOOMSBURY ABSOLUTE
LONDON · OXFORD · NEW YORK · NEW DELHI · SYDNEY

BLOOMSBURY ABSOLUTE
Bloomsbury Publishing Plc
50 Bedford Square, London, WC1B 3DP, UK
29 Earlsfort Terrace, Dublin 2, Ireland

BLOOMSBURY, BLOOMSBURY ABSOLUTE, the Diana logo and the Absolute Press logo are trademarks of Bloomsbury Publishing Plc

First published in Great Britain 2021

A catalogue record for this book is available from the British Library.

Library of Congress Cataloguing-in-Publication data has been applied for.

HB: 9781472983039
ePUB: 9781472983046
ePDF: 9781472983053

33614082478867

2 4 6 8 10 9 7 5 3 1

Printed in China by RRD Asia Printing Solutions Limited.

MIX
Paper from responsible sources
FSC® C144853

To find out more about our authors and books visit www.bloomsbury.com and sign up for our newsletters.

Ch. 1   Introduction

How it all started

One Christmastime I stood in the kitchen at Djurgårdsbrunn's Värdshus having prepared a feast of more than 50 types of delicacy for friends and family. For most of our guests, it was the festivities and the chance to socialise that attracted them, but of course the food was important too.

Out of all the dishes I'd made, it was the meatballs that were the most popular, virtually disappearing before my eyes. And so began the dream: a restaurant and shop where everything is about the humble meatball. Ten months later, we opened Meatballs for the People. It was 2013.

My background

Not many people can say it, but I'm living my dream life. I'm in the middle of my life and my days are all about family, food, drink and life in the restaurants.

I started in the industry at a young age as an apprentice in a kitchen under a classically trained, French-schooled chef. It was there that I learned that the guest is always the most important thing in a restaurant, and that you have to make an effort if you want to progress in the kitchen, otherwise you never get away from peeling potatoes.

I have had the great fortune to work in several of the best, award-winning restaurants in Stockholm over the years, and I have competed with the Swedish Culinary Olympic team, which resulted in several successes and a gold medal in 2000. This gave me the confidence and ability to do what I think most chefs dream of, and, along with two friends, we started our first restaurant in 2003: Bockholmen Hav & Restaurang on Stockholm's archipelago. When we first opened there was an elegant dish of venison meatballs on the menu, the first meatball dish on my own menu. Over the years there have been several more restaurants, including Meatballs for the People, which all have a special place in my chef's heart.

When we opened Meatballs for the People, we didn't know how it would be received, but we couldn't have predicted that a restaurant serving only meatballs would turn out to be such a success. We are now open every day of the week, for lunch and dinner, offering takeaways and deliveries, and we always have at least twelve kinds of meatball on the menu.

When it comes to festivities and festivals, we really push the boat out, with some special lamb meatballs for Easter, for example. At MFTP, you buy the tastiest lingonberries and eat meatballs you did not think existed. Our guests are both locals and tourists coming from further afield. I would never have imagined that Swedish meatballs would attract so many guests from all over the world, but today we are, for many, a natural part of a visit to Stockholm, something I'm very proud of, as we get to share an important piece of Swedish food culture.

The importance of Swedish meatballs

The meatball has been mentioned in Swedish gastronomy since the 1700s. It has been said that King Charles XII spent several years in what is now Bendery in Moldova, then under Turkish rule, and returned to Sweden in 1715 armed with a recipe for meatballs.

The classic Swedish meatballs is typically smaller than those you will find across Europe, and are traditionally made with a 50:50 mix of pork and beef, and flavoured with spices such as allspice or nutmeg, something we've kept true to in our Classic Meatballs for the People recipe (see page 18). The Swedish meatball is also particularly revered for its smooth texture, which is achieved by beating the meatball mixture rather than using your hands to just bring the ingredients together.

THIS MACHINE WAS THE BEGINNING OF EVERYTHING

While everyone's heard of the Swedish meatball, you also find meatballs all over the world, in some form or other: they can be big in Italy, small and elegant in Thailand or spicy in India, but the tradition of serving some kind of minced meat shaped to spheres is common in many countries. If I had to choose, other than the Swedish meatball, of course, my favourite would be Greek meatballs (known as koftas) with feta cheese, preferably enjoyed at a taverna somewhere near the Mediterranean.

Meatballs tend to pop up all over the place in Sweden, whether it's something quick to make for dinner or leftovers cold in a sandwich (or on our traditional open sandwiches), but there is no meatball as good as the one you had as a child, cooked by someone you love – your mother or maybe your grandfather. I remember my grandmother's meatballs; they were something I longed for, and were a treat when it came to family dinners. We Swedes love all forms of meatballs, but nothing beats homemade.

As a dish, meatballs are something that suits almost all restaurants, and in Sweden it is something that sells well on any menu. You can make them fancy or keep them classic, but people are always happy to see them on a menu and order something they know and love. Meatballs for the People has a van that we use for local deliveries and take to farmers' markets. I love how creative we can be with the recipes that we offer from the van or the restaurant, serving a huge range of flavours, but still all meatballs.

When I come across a range of ingredients or experience different flavours, I often think about how those flavours would work in a meatball, which is why there's a chapter on meatballs from around the world, using my favourite flavours from all corners of the globe. I have enjoyed hundreds of different meatballs over the years, at the restaurant and at home, and my favourites have been gathered here.

So, what makes good meatball?

For me it is about two things. Firstly, you must make them with good ingredients (so buy local, sustainably and seasonally, when possible). Secondly, you must like the person or restaurant that cooked your meatballs: a meatball from a food factory will never be as good as ones your children cook for you.

When it comes to taste and texture, some people like when the meatball falls apart and might be a little dry, while others like juicy meatballs, like the ones we serve at MFTP, packed full of flavour. Freshly fried or cooked in sauce, it's just a matter of taste.

I use higher-fat mince in our meatballs, as it creates a juicier and tastier ball. Fat makes food taste better! When mixing the ingredients, I add salt from the start, as it breaks down the meat a little and helps bind all the ingredients together. It's also very important that all the ingredients are cold when you start combining them for your meatballs.

A meatball will always be a meatball, but you can of course make lovely vegetarian and fish balls, and serve them in the same way as meatballs. We offer veggie meatballs at the restaurant (and three of our favourites feature in this book), and I believe that if meat does not taste better than a falafel from my local falafel bar, then go veggie. But when we choose to eat meat, it must be done respectfully and be of really good quality.

When we opened MFTP, it was my belief that we would always know where our meat came from, right down to the breeders, and that we would only use the best quality. We have the world's best butcher and fishmonger who we source our ingredients from. In him, I have made a friend for life, and this book features a recipe inspired from a trip we made to Spain, looking for good ingredients and suppliers.

What goes best with meatballs

There is a huge range of sides dishes and sauces that are delicious with meatballs, from the classic lingonberries, potatoes and cream sauce, to cranberry ketchup and cucumber pickles – it's a matter of personal preference, so take your pick! All the recipes in the final chapter of this book are for you to mix and match with any of the main dishes – we love to add pickles to any meal.

When it comes to drinks, I think that beer is the best accompaniment to meatballs. At MFTP we collaborate with Gotlands Brewery, a company that cherishes fine craftsmanship: we like that! We also make a lingonberry drink with sparkling water which is hugely popular – the secret is finding the perfect balance between sweetness and acidity. We are also lucky enough to have a gin distillery in our neighbourhood, Stockholms Bränneri, which we use for both cooking and magically good drinks.

Notes on the recipes

It is always best to eat your meatballs freshly made, but if you have leftovers they will keep in the fridge for a couple of days, or you can freeze them for up to a month, just make sure they freeze quickly. To reheat, simply fry in a little butter until hot through.

Meatballs can be made and enjoyed in a variety of sizes. For home cooking, I often to make them about 30g each, about the size of a table tennis ball, but if you make them bigger, they stay juicier longer and take on a more rustic feel, which is why at the restaurant we usually make them about 45g. And if you make them smaller, they become more elegant and are great for dinner parties and small children.

Always use the best ingredients you can, and try to source local where possible. If you cannot find some ingredients, I've suggested alternatives here:

Bear	venison: shoulder, brisket or neck
Cloudberries	redcurrants
Dill seeds	fennel seeds
Elk	venison: shoulder, brisket or neck
Lingonberries	redcurrants
Lingonberry juice	unsweetened cranberry juice
Pickled herrings	marinated herrings
Pickled anchovies	ordinary anchovy fillets in oil
Reindeer	venison or lean beef: neck or shoulder

- Use medium eggs.
- Teaspoon and tablespoon measures are level.
- A good temperature for keeping meatballs warm while frying in batches is 140°C/Fan 120°C/Gas 1.

Ch. 2   Our Best Balls

Classic Meatballs for the People

This is the classic Swedish meatball recipe – served at parties and small suppers, for children and adults alike. This is how we in Sweden love our meatballs. I can, and do, eat ten of these meatballs in one sitting! It's also our signature dish at Meatballs for the People.

Here I've chosen to pair these ever-popular meatballs with a sophisticated red wine sauce, but for a more casual supper Cream Sauce (page 58) is a traditional choice.

Making the perfect mashed potatoes – an essential accompaniment – is an art, and recipes can only be a guide. So much depends on what type of potatoes you use, what time of year it is and how you boil the potatoes, but when you get all the variables right, the result is magical. And, I urge you not to be tempted to use a food processor. The blades break down the starch cells in the potatoes, and the result is a gloopy mess. Even in the restaurant we use a potato ricer or old-fashioned hand masher to guarantee light, fluffy butter-rich mash.

Serves 4–6; makes about 38 balls, depending on the size

500g beef mince
500g pork mince
I egg, beaten
1½ tablespoons sea salt
I teaspoon ground allspice
freshly ground white pepper
100ml whipping cream
50g onion, finely chopped, fried in butter until soft then chilled
butter, for frying
Classic Lingonberries (page 115) or Grandpa's Lingonberries (page 116) or Finger Cucumber (page 19), to serve, optional

1 Beat the beef and pork minces with the egg, salt and allspice and white pepper in a large mixing bowl with a wooden spoon until firmer. Add the cream and onion and continue beating until the mixture is smooth, firm, well combined and forms a big meatball. Cover and chill in the fridge for at least 1 hour.

2 Meanwhile, make the wine sauce and mashed potatoes. To make the sauce, melt the butter in a large heavy-based saucepan over a low heat. Add the onion and fry, stirring occasionally, for about 10 minutes until softened and beginning to brown. Add the sugar, increase the heat to medium and stir until the onions have caramelised and browned.

3 Add the wine and stock to the pan and bring to the boil, stirring to loosen any sediment on the bottom of the pan. Reduce the heat and simmer, uncovered, for about 30 minutes until the sauce is reduced by half.

Ingredients and method continued on page 20

For the barolo wine sauce

50g butter
1 red onion, sliced
1 teaspoon brown sugar
1 bottle (750ml) great
 Barolo wine
1 litre oxtail or beef stock
sea salt and freshly ground
 black pepper
2 tablespoons cornflour,
 mixed to a paste with
 1½ tablespoons water

For the Swedish mashed potatoes

sea salt
1kg floury potatoes, peeled
250g butter, melted and kept hot
about 250ml whipping cream,
 warm

4 When the sauce has reduced, season with salt and pepper to taste. Stir in the cornflour mixture, slowly bring to the boil, stirring, until it has thickened slightly. Strain the sauce and keep hot, or reheat just before serving.

5 While the sauce is simmering, prepare the mashed potatoes. Bring a saucepan of salted water to the boil and add the potatoes. Boil until the potatoes are cooked through but not breaking apart. Drain well, then let them steam dry in the saucepan until they are really dry. Pass the potatoes through a potato ricer into a large bowl, or use a hand masher. Add the butter and stir until the potatoes and butter are thoroughly mixed. Add half of the cream and continue stirring until combined. If you want a softer texture, add more cream. Finish by tasting and seasoning with salt. Set aside and keep hot until ready to serve.

6 Once the meat mixture has chilled, roll it into smooth balls, of whatever size you choose (page 14). This quantity makes about 38 smooth balls, each 30g and the size of a table tennis ball.

7 Melt enough butter in a large frying pan over a medium heat to come about one-third of the way up the meatballs. Add as many meatballs as will fit, without overcrowding, and fry, turning frequently, for about 15 minutes until brown on the outside and cooked through when you cut one open. Pan-fry in batches, if necessary. As each batch is fried, use a slotted spoon to transfer it to a baking tray and keep hot.

8 Just before serving, reheat the sauce, if necessary. Serve the meatballs, mash and sauce on plates, with any extra sauce on the side for guests to help themselves.

Deer Balls

with a seven-spice sauce

This dish is a favourite in autumn, when warming, hearty and spicy recipes are very welcome. Serve with a red wine with a lot of flavour, preferably one aged in oak barrels. It's important to use a veal mince with the highest fat content you can buy, to counter the leanness of the venison mince.

The spice mix makes more than you need, but it's difficult to mix in smaller quantities, so store it in airtight container. It would also be good for flavouring the potatoes in Seaman's Steak Balls (page 51).

Serves 4–6; makes about 40 balls

vegetable oil for greasing
700g venison mince
300g veal mince, with the highest
    fat content you can buy
4 teaspoons sea salt
1 tablespoon finely chopped
    fresh tarragon
200ml whipping cream
butter, for frying
pickled onions, to serve
    (optional)
seeded rye bread, to serve
    (optional)

For the pumpkin two ways

2 pumpkins or butternut
    squashes, about 1kg each,
    halved lengthwise
sea salt
500ml crème fraîche

1   First prepare the pumpkins. Preheat the oven to 200°C/Fan 180°C/Gas 6, and grease a baking sheet. Put the pumpkin halves on the baking sheet and roast, skin-side up, until they feel soft. Depending on their size, this will take about 45 minutes. The pumpkins should take on colour, but not burn. Remove them from the oven.

2   Cut one pumpkin half into at least one wedge per diner, leaving the seeds attached – they are both beautiful and delicious – then return the wedges to the baking sheet and set aside. When cool enough to handle, scrape the flesh from the remaining pumpkin into a saucepan, discarding the skin and seeds, and leave over a very low heat to warm on the hob for 1 hour, stirring occasionally. The pumpkin should be as dry as possible, without catching and burning on the bottom of the pan.

3   Meanwhile, prepare the spices for the sauce and make the meatballs. Grind the cinnamon, star anise, allspice, cardamom, chilli flakes, cloves and fennel seeds with the bay leaves in a spice blender or coffee grinder. The spices should be well ground, but still have some structure left. Stir thoroughly to combine.

Ingredients and method continued on page 23

For the seven spice sauce
3cm piece cinnamon stick
3 pieces star anise
1½ teaspoons allspice berries
1½ teaspoons green cardamom
   pods
½ teaspoon red chilli flakes
1½ teaspoons whole cloves
1½ teaspoons fennel seeds
2 fresh bay leaves
600ml veal or beef gravy – you
   want a really strong flavour
50g butter, diced
sea salt

4   To make the meatballs, beat the venison and veal minces with the salt and tarragon in a large mixing bowl, using a wooden spoon, until the minces are combined and firmer. Add the cream and continue beating until the mixture is smooth, firm and well combined. Shape the mixture into about 40 smooth meatballs, each 30g and the size of a table tennis ball. Set aside until ready to cook.

5   When the pumpkin flesh is dry, blend the flesh with the crème fraîche until smooth, then season with sea salt. Set aside until ready to serve.

6   Melt enough butter in a large frying pan over a medium heat to come about one-third of the way up the meatballs. Add as many meatballs as will fit, without overcrowding, and fry, turning frequently, for about 10 minutes until brown on the outside and cooked through when you cut one open. Pan-fry in batches, if necessary. As each batch is fried, use a slotted spoon to transfer it to a baking tray and keep hot.

7   Meanwhile, reheat the pumpkin wedges in the oven at 170°C/Fan 150°C/Gas 3 and make the sauce. Heat the veal gravy over a high heat. Add 1 teaspoon of the spice mix, taste and add more if you like. Add the butter and blitz with a stick blender until the sauce becomes glossy and a little thicker. Season with salt, if necessary.

8   To serve, add a pumpkin wedge and a spoonful of pumpkin purée to each plate, then pile on the meatballs. Pour over the spicy sauce, and, if using, add a couple of pickled onion pieces to help balance the spices in the sauce. A good, dark seeded rye bread makes a perfect accompaniment.

Elk on Fire

with green peppercorns

 In Sweden, the elk is king of the woods. Every autumn during hunting season we have access to fresh elk meat – then it is elk meatballs for the people at the restaurant. Out of season, or when elk meat just isn't available, substitute with venison.

Makes about 40 balls

700g boneless elk meat, finely
   minced
300g veal mince, with the highest
   fat content you can buy
1½ tablespoons sea salt
800ml whipping cream
70g green peppercorns in brine,
   drained – 20g chopped and
   50g left whole
rapeseed oil, for frying
about 5 tablespoons Cognac
   or other brandy, to flambé –
   the one in the photo is my
   favourite
sea salt
Colourful Carrots with Mustard
   Seeds (page 127), to serve
boiled potatoes, to serve

1 Beat the elk and veal minces with the salt in a large mixing bowl with a wooden spoon until the minces are combined and firmer. Add 200ml of the cream and chopped peppercorns and continue beating until the mixture is smooth, firm and well combined. Transfer the bowl to the fridge for 15 minutes to chill before shaping the meatballs.

2 Shape the mixture into about 40 smooth meatballs, 30g each and the size of a table tennis ball.

3 Heat a thin layer of rapeseed oil in a very large frying pan over a medium heat. Add as many meatballs as will fit, without overcrowding, and fry, turning frequently, for about 10 minutes until brown on the outside and cooked through when you cut one open. Pan-fry in batches. As each batch is fried, use a slotted spoon to transfer it to a baking tray and keep hot.

4 When all the meatballs are cooked, return them to the pan. Raise the heat and when it is really hot, pour over your favourite Cognac and set it alight; use a lighter if it does not catch fire immediately. Add the whole green peppercorns after the flames die down and stir in the remaining cream. Let the meatballs simmer in the cream sauce for 2–3 minutes, then add a little more Cognac if you want stronger-tasting sauce. Adjust the seasoning, if necessary.

5 Place the frying pan directly on a heatproof mat on the table to serve. The sauce should be gently bubbling so the scent of green peppercorns and Cognac spreads across in the room. Serve with the carrots and freshly boiled potatoes.

Reindeer Balls

in horseradish cream

 Horseradish is a distant cousin to mustard, and both go well with wild meat. When I was a young kid we would often have sandwiches filled with reindeer and creamy horseradish for picnics, which is where my inspiration here comes from. You don't need much juniper, as it's a strong taste – and for anyone who loves gin, it's a familiar one!

Makes about 40 balls

700g reindeer mince
300g veal mince, with the highest
    fat content you can buy
4 teaspoons sea salt
200ml whipping cream
I tablespoon juniper berries,
    finely crushed
freshly ground white pepper
butter, for frying
oven-roasted new potatoes,
    to serve
pickled cucumber (pages 119
    and 120), to serve
finely chopped flat-leaf parsley,
    to garnish

For the horseradish cream
750ml whipping cream
I½ teaspoons Dijon mustard
grated fresh horseradish – I like
    to use a lot – plus extra,
    to garnish
75g butter
sea salt

1   Beat the reindeer and veal minces with the salt in a large mixing bowl, using a wooden spoon, until the minces combine and become firmer. Beat in the cream and crushed juniper berries, season with white pepper and continue beating until the mixture is smooth, firm and well combined. Shape the mixture into about 40 smooth meatballs, each 30g and the size of a table tennis ball.

2   Melt enough butter in a frying pan over a medium heat to come about one-third of the way up the meatballs. Add as many balls as will fit, without overcrowding, and fry, turning frequently, for about 10 minutes until brown on the outside and cooked through when you cut one open. Pan-fry in batches, if necessary. As each batch is fried, use a slotted spoon to transfer it to a baking tray and keep hot.

3   While the meatballs are cooking, make the horseradish cream. Put the cream, Dijon mustard and 1½ tablespoons grated horseradish, or to taste, in a saucepan and bring to the boil. Reduce the heat and simmer, uncovered, for 5 minutes. Remove the pan from the heat and whisk in the butter until the sauce is glossier and little thicker. Season with salt to taste.

4   Pour plenty of sauce on to serving plates, top with the reindeer balls and serve with oven-roasted potatoes and pickled cucumber alongside. Finish by grating over horseradish and sprinkling with parsley. Serve with any leftover horseradish sauce in a jug at the table – there's always someone who loves the punchy flavours.

Brown Bear and Sweet Cloudberry Balls

We Swedes love these meatballs, which contain something really exotic, even for us in Scandinavia — a wild meat absolutely full of flavour. I don't use any extra spices, other than sea salt and a little white pepper for these morsels, because I want the taste of the wilderness to come through. These are great served simply with some hasselback potatoes and a chilled beer.

Makes about 40 balls

500g black bear mince
500g veal mince, at least 12% fat
4 teaspoons sea salt
200ml whipping cream
freshly ground white pepper
butter, for frying
300g cloudberries, thawed if
    frozen
100ml concentrated beef stock
Hasselback Potatoes (page 132),
    to serve, optional

1   Beat the bear and veal minces with the salt in a large mixing bowl, using a wooden spoon, until the two minces are combined and the mixture is firmer. Add the cream and a couple of turns of the peppermill and continue beating until the mixture is smooth, firm and well combined. Shape the mixture into about 40 smooth meatballs, each 30g and the size of a table tennis ball.

2   Melt enough butter in a large frying pan over a medium heat to come about one-third of the way up the meatballs. Add as many meatballs as will fit, without overcrowding, and fry, turning frequently, for 10–15 minutes until brown on the outside and cooked through when you cut one open. Pan-fry in batches, if necessary. As each batch is fried, use a slotted spoon to transfer it to a baking tray and keep hot.

3   When all the meatballs are cooked, return them to the pan and spoon over the hot butter. Add the cloudberries, shaking the pan; the butter will sizzle thoroughly. Pour in the beef stock and shake the pan a few times to heat the meatballs and the sauce through.

4   To serve, transfer everything to a warm serving platter or plates, so the meatballs are swimming in sweet cloudberries and the nutty melted butter with a little beef stock. Serve with the potatoes, if using.

Pork and Black Pudding Balls

with lingonberry cream

For this recipe I have taken inspiration from a Swedish classic, black pudding served with lingonberry jam. It is delicious on its own, but add boiled potatoes if you are really hungry.

Serves 6–8; makes about 46 balls

1kg pork mince
1 egg, beaten
1½ tablespoons sea salt
1 teaspoon dried oregano
50g sultanas, chopped
100ml whipping cream
freshly ground white pepper
200g black pudding, casing removed and broken into fine pieces
butter, for frying

For the lingonberry cream
500ml whipping cream
100g lingonberries, thawed if frozen and finely chopped

To serve
20 Brussels sprouts, trimmed
1 crisp, sweet apple, cut into fine sticks
handful of lingonberries

1   First prepare the lingonberry cream. Put the cream in a bowl and whisk until it begins to thicken. Add the lingonberries and continue whisking until it becomes a lovely pink colour and holds soft peaks when the whisk is lifted. Cover and chill until ready to serve.

2   To make the balls, beat the mince, egg and salt in a large mixing bowl with a wooden spoon until the mince becomes firmer. Add the oregano, sultanas and cream, season with white pepper and continue beating until the mixture is smooth, firm and well combined. Finally, gently stir in the black pudding until distributed throughout. If the mixture is too firm, stir in a little cold water to loosen. Shape the mixture into about 46 smooth meatballs, each 30g and the size of a table tennis ball.

3   Melt enough butter in a large frying pan over a medium heat to come about one-third of the way up the meatballs. Add as many meatballs as will fit, without overcrowding, and fry, turning frequently, for about 10 minutes until brown on the outside and cooked through when you cut one open. Pan-fry in batches, if necessary. Be careful when you fry these, as it can be difficult to see the difference between burnt and the colour of black pudding. As each batch is fried, use a slotted spoon to transfer it to a baking tray and keep hot.

4   Meanwhile, bring a pan of salted water to the boil. Add the Brussels sprouts and blanch for 5 minutes, or until tender. Drain and keep hot.

5   Arrange the pork balls and Brussels sprouts on plates and add dollops of the lingonberry cream. Scatter round the apple and a few extra lingonberries and serve.

Smokey and the Pig

with cheesy pasta

Pork and smoke are a great combination, and when you add pasta and cheese you're on to a winner. I am a big fan of all types of cheese, which is one of the reasons I'm so fond of this dish! It's also ideal for casual entertaining at home. My favourite pasta shape for this recipe is the really big shells, which crisp in the oven.

Serves 6–8; makes about 46 balls

900g pork mince
100g smoked bacon, rind
   removed, and finely chopped
1 egg, beaten
200ml whipping cream
freshly ground black pepper
butter, for frying

For the cheesy pasta
3 eggs
500ml milk
500ml whipping cream
2 teaspoons sea salt
1 teaspoon freshly grated nutmeg
600g pasta, cooked for 2 minutes
   less than specified on the
   packet and well drained
200g Cheddar cheese, grated

To serve
watercress sprigs
goat's cheese, crumbled
Cranberry Ketchup (page 135)

1 First prepare the pasta. Preheat the oven to 200°C/Fan 180°C/Gas 6. Beat the eggs together in a bowl, then stir in the milk and cream. Add the salt and nutmeg. Stir in the cooked pasta until well blended. Transfer to a large flat pan or ovenproof serving dish, and spread out so some of the pasta sticks up from the egg mixture. Sprinkle over the Cheddar cheese and bake for about 30 minutes until beginning to brown. If the pasta starts to get too much colour, cover with a piece of foil; the pasta should be creamy on the bottom and crisp on top.

2 Meanwhile, make the pork balls. Beat the pork and bacon together in a large bowl, using a wooden spoon, until firmer; the salt in the bacon acts as a binder. Add the egg and beat for a few more minutes, then beat in the cream and add a couple hefty turns of the peppermill. Continue beating until the mixture is smooth, firm and well combined. Shape the mix into about 46 smooth meatballs, 30g each and the size of a table tennis ball.

3 Melt enough butter in a large frying pan over a medium heat to come about one-third of the way up the meatballs. Add as many meatballs as will fit, without overcrowding, and fry, turning frequently, for 10–15 minutes until brown on the outside and cooked through when you cut one open. Pan-fry in batches, if necessary. As each batch is fried, use a slotted spoon to transfer it to a baking tray and keep hot.

4 To serve, arrange the meatballs on a plate, with the watercress and goat's cheese scattered around, and plenty of cranberry ketchup for adding at the table. Serve with the pasta straight from the oven.

Jamaican Rooster Balls

and a crisp Caesar salad

 Most of my recipes are pan-fried, but I roast these chicken balls. You can, if you want, fry them in butter, but it's a bit more difficult because the mince becomes very soft and the balls easily lose their shape.

Serves 4–6; makes about 36 balls

700g boneless, skinless chicken
   breasts and thighs, minced
4 teaspoons sea salt
400ml whipping cream
2 tablespoons grated lime zest
1 teaspoon ground allspice
1 teaspoon red chilli flakes
½ teaspoon ground cinnamon
½ small nutmeg, grated
1 tablespoon finely chopped
   fresh coriander
butter, for frying the lime halves
2–3 limes, halved, to serve
2 heads cos lettuce, halved
   lengthwise, to serve
extra red chilli flakes, to garnish

For the Caesar dressing
400g mayonnaise
12g anchovies, preferably
   smoked, chopped
4 tablespoons sherry vinegar
200g Parmesan cheese, grated,
   plus extra, to serve
freshly ground black pepper

1   Beat the mince with the salt in a large mixing bowl, using a wooden spoon, until it is firmer, which should take a couple of minutes. Add the cream, lime zest, allspice, chilli flakes, cinnamon, nutmeg and coriander, and continue beating until the mixture is smooth, firm and well combined. Chill in the fridge for at least 1 hour before shaping into balls.

2   Meanwhile, prepare the Caesar salad dressing. Mix the mayonnaise, anchovies, vinegar and Parmesan together, and finish with a couple of turns of the peppermill. Cover and chill if not using immediately.

3   Preheat the oven to 200°C/Fan 180°C/Gas 6.

4   When you are ready to cook, shape the mixture into about 36 smooth meatballs, each 30g and the size of a table tennis ball. Place on a baking tray and roast for 20–25 minutes, turning once, until they are lightly browned and cooked through when you cut one open.

5   Meanwhile, melt a little butter in a frying pan. Add the lime halves, cut-sides down, and fry until they caramelise.

6   To serve, put a hearty dollop of the Caesar dressing on individual plates and add the salad halves. Add the balls to the plates with the lime halves. Sprinkle with freshly grated Parmesan and a few chilli flakes, then serve.

Chunky Salmon Balls

in red and black pearls with Sandefjord Sauce

In Sweden we have a long tradition of eating salmon, which is a very popular source of protein. The salmon we have in our seas have white meat, but I often use salmon from Norway, which is beautiful in its colour and lovely in taste. You need to handle salmon gently, and don't overcook it or it will become dull and dry.

The classic Scandinavian butter-and-caviar sauce is perfect to serve alongside little fishy balls.

Serves 4–6; makes about 32 balls

1kg salmon fillet, skinned
1 teaspoon ground cumin
1 teaspoon ground fennel, or
   1¼ teaspoons fennel seeds,
   finely crushed
2 tablespoons sea salt
2 teaspoons sugar
butter, for frying

For the carrot pickle
3 heritage carrots in a variety
   of colours, peeled and thinly
   shaved
100ml Ättika Pickling Liquid
   (page 112)
3 crown dill sprigs, or fresh dill
   sprigs, plus extra to serve

1   Chop the salmon into small pieces – some should be more finely chopped than others so you have a slightly chunky mixture.

2   Mix the salmon in a bowl with the cumin, fennel, salt and sugar until the mixture becomes firmer; the salt makes the salmon quite firm. Once everything is combined, cover and leave to rest in the fridge for 1–2 hours.

3   While the mixture is chilling, prepare the carrot pickle. Mix the carrots with the Ättika Pickling Liquid, like a salad, and finish with the crown dill sprigs. Set aside until ready to serve.

4   When the salmon mixture has chilled, with dampened hands, shape the mixture into about 32 smooth balls, each 30g and the size of a table tennis ball.

5   Melt enough butter in a large frying pan over a medium heat to come about one-third of the way up the meatballs. Add as many meatballs as will fit, without overcrowding, and quickly fry, turning frequently, for a few minutes, until cooked to your liking. These do not need to be cooked completely through; in fact, I like the centres a little rare.

Ingredients and method continued on page 38

For the Sandefjord sauce

300g butter, diced
300ml whipping cream
300g crème fraîche
100g mixture of your favourite
   caviars, such as salmon, trout
   or sturgeon

Pan-fry in batches, if necessary. As each batch is fried, use a slotted spoon to transfer it to a baking tray and keep hot.

6   Meanwhile, prepare the sauce. Put the butter, cream and crème fraîche in a saucepan and bring to the boil, whisking so it becomes a smooth sauce. Cover and keep hot until the salmon balls are cooked.

7   Just before serving, stir the caviar into the sauce.

8   Spoon the sauce on to warmed plates, add the salmon balls, and top with the pickled carrot. Garnish with crown dill sprigs.

Sweet Potato and Corn Balls

The challenge with these balls is to get the sweet potato mixture really dry and firm, otherwise you cannot fry the balls without them falling apart. Have fun!

Makes about 36 balls

butter, for frying the shallots and the balls
200g shallots, roughly chopped
1kg sweet potatoes – I like to use both orange and white – peeled and roughly diced
about 1 litre vegetable stock
200g corn kernels, thawed and well drained, if frozen
300g Parmesan cheese, finely grated, plus extra, to garnish
sea salt
about 70g panko breadcrumbs

To serve
2 corn cobs, thinly sliced lengthwise a couple of times
1 large broccoli head, divided into florets and the stalks thinly sliced
sriracha chilli sauce
3 tablespoons mayonnaise

1 Melt enough butter to form a shallow layer in a large, deep frying pan over a medium heat. Add the shallots and fry for about 8 minutes until soft, but not coloured. Add the sweet potatoes and enough vegetable stock to just cover them. Bring to the boil, then lower the heat and simmer, uncovered, over a medium-high heat. Let the sweet potatoes cook slowly, adding a little more stock after a while if they start looking too dry, for about 15 minutes. Think of it like simmering a risotto.

2 When the sweet potatoes are soft, stir in the corn kernels with a wooden spoon and continue stirring and breaking up the potatoes until the liquid evaporates and the mixture reduces to a pulp. When you think it is ready, cook for a further 5 minutes, stirring, to really make sure the mixture is dry. It is important that all the liquid evaporates, as otherwise the balls will be too soggy to hold their shape while being fried. Finish by stirring in the Parmesan; you should now have a firm sweet potato pulp. Season with salt to taste. (It's important to salt last, as the Parmesan cheese and possibly the stock are salty.) Let the mix cool thoroughly; it will thicken as it cools.

3 When the mixture is cold, shape it into about 36 smooth meatballs, each 30g and the size of a table tennis ball. Roll the balls in panko breadcrumbs so each is well coated. It's important they are properly coated, as this makes them extra crispy when fried.

4 Melt enough butter in a large frying pan over a low to come about one-third of the way up the meatballs. Add as many meatballs as will fit, without overcrowding, and fry gently to prevent them from burning

Continued on page 41

on the bottom of the pan, turning frequently, for about 5 minutes until brown on the outside and cooked through when you cut one open. Pan-fry in batches, if necessary. As each batch is fried, use a slotted spoon to transfer it to a baking tray and keep hot.

5   Meanwhile, blanch the corn cobs and the broccoli florets and stalks in boiling salted water for 1–2 minutes until just tender, but still retaining some bite. Stir a little sriracha through the mayonnaise.

6   Arrange the sweet potato balls on a plate with the cooked vegetables and add a little of the sriracha-mayo and a few splashes of pure sriracha. Sprinkle over extra Parmesan cheese to garnish, and serve with extra sriracha on the table.

Ch. 3　Meatballs at Home

Open Bear Ball Sandwiches

with beetroot salad

Meatballs and beetroot salad is something that is served everywhere in Sweden. Sometimes you just want a good lovely sandwich, and this is on the top-ten list for me.

When I'm using shop-bought mayonnaise for the beetroot salad, I stir in a little Dijon mustard to boost the flavour.

Serves 6; makes 6 balls

150g bear or venison mince
150g veal mince, with the highest
    fat content you can buy
1 teaspoon sea salt
1 egg
½ teaspoon ground juniper (use
    less if you want a milder taste)
½ teaspoon finely chopped
    rosemary needles
1 tablespoon whipping cream
butter, for frying

For the beetroot salad
300g pickled beetroot, diced
200g mayonnaise

To serve
6 slices coarse rye bread,
    preferably made with some
    dried fruit
6 small Cos lettuce leaves, or any
    other crisp salad leaves
½ yellow beetroot, peeled and
    thinly sliced

1   Beat both minces with the salt, egg, juniper and rosemary in a large mixing bowl with a wooden spoon until the minces are combined and the mixture becomes firmer. Add the cream and continue beating until the mixture is smooth and well combined; it should have a soft consistency. Shape the mixture into 6 smooth meatballs, each 60g. Set aside.

2   To make the beetroot salad, mix the beetroot with the mayonnaise – I like when it is nice and creamy with pieces of beetroot for texture. It should be a beautiful pink colour.

3   Melt enough butter in a large frying pan over a medium heat to come about one-third of the way up the meatballs. Add as many meatballs as will fit, without overcrowding, and fry, turning frequently, for about 18 minutes until brown on the outside and cooked through when you cut one open. Pan-fry in batches, if necessary. As each batch is fried, use a slotted spoon to transfer it to a baking tray and keep hot until all are fried.

4   To serve, assemble the open sandwiches with the rye bread, lettuce leaves and yellow beetroot, topped with a warm meatball. This way you get plenty of beetroot salad with every bite, which is super tasty.

Jack's Samurai Pork Meatballs

These meatballs are one of several I had on the original Meatballs for the People menu that I thought would appeal to children, as well as their parents. We don't put meatballs specifically for children on the menu, but my instinct has proved correct and this is one of the favourites for all generations. It's named after my son, Jack, who at the time was still a baby and had no idea about samurai! Some airy jasmine rice goes particularly nicely with these.

Makes about 36 balls

sunflower oil, for greasing the baking tray and frying
1kg pork mince, preferably 20% fat for the best pork flavour
2 teaspoons sea salt
1 egg, beaten
20g sushi ginger, finely shredded
100ml Japanese oyster sauce
100g tomato ketchup
4 teaspoons toasted sesame seeds
Cos lettuce hearts, or any other crisp leaves, to serve

1 Preheat the oven to 200°C/Fan 180°C/Gas 6, and lightly grease a baking tray large enough to hold all the meatballs in a single layer.

2 Beat the mince with the salt in a large mixing bowl with a wooden spoon until firmer. Beat in the egg and sushi ginger until it is smooth, firm and well combined. Add a little cold water if the mixture feels too firm. Shape the mixture into about 36 smooth meatballs, each 30g and the size of a table tennis ball.

3 Place each on the greased baking tray as it is shaped. Roast for 10 minutes, or until they are cooked through when you cut one open.

4 Meanwhile, mix together the oyster sauce and tomato ketchup.

5 When the meatballs are cooked, heat a thin layer of oil in a very large frying pan over a medium-high heat. Add all the meatballs and fry, turning frequently, for about 2 minutes, until brown all over. Lower the heat, add the oyster sauce and ketchup mixture to the pan and gently stir for a minute or two; they should be perfectly shiny and sticky. It's important that the glaze doesn't burn, boil dry or split, so keep a close eye on it. Once the meatballs are glazed, sprinkle them with sesame seeds.

6 These are best eaten with your hands, using a lettuce leaf as a cup for the meatballs and sauce.

Grandma's Meatballs

To experience memories through food is a great feeling, and to pass on a tradition is just as wonderful, which is why this recipe is so special to me. These meatballs – exactly like my grandmother used to make – have a rougher structure than most I make and serve today. I hope you agree these are particularly nice. A couple of cooked, peeled potatoes are always a welcome accompaniment if you're hungry.

Makes about 42 balls

500g beef mince
500g pork mince
1 egg, beaten
1 teaspoon ground allspice
1 teaspoon ground ginger
1 teaspoon sea salt
freshly ground white pepper
50g boiled and peeled floury
    potato, mashed and left to
    cool completely
100ml whipping cream
100g onion, chopped
butter, for frying

To serve
Classic Lingonberries (page 115)
Cauliflower Pickles in Pink Gin
    (page 124)
Sweet Parsley Cucumber
    (page 123)

1 Beat both minces with the egg, allspice, ginger, salt, white pepper to taste and the potato in a large mixing bowl with a wooden spoon until firmer. Add the cream and give the mixture a couple of quick stirs; it should have a soft consistency. Finally, stir in the onion and continue beating until the mixture is smooth, firm and well combined. Shape the mixture into about 42 meatballs, 30g each and the size of a table tennis ball; there will be a few onion pieces sticking out.

2 Melt enough butter in a large frying pan over a medium heat to come about one-third of the way up the meatballs. Add as many meatballs as will fit, without overcrowding, and fry, turning frequently, for about 10 minutes until brown on the outside and cooked through when you cut one open. It is important that the heat in the pan does not get too hot, or the small onion pieces will break off and burn. A couple of the meatballs might even break a bit, but that is okay. Pan-fry in batches, if necessary. As each batch is fried use a slotted spoon to transfer it to an ovenproof serving dish and keep hot.

3 I like to serve these meatballs with the butter they are cooked in with any onion pieces that have fallen off in the frying pan. I always think these are best eaten with a lot of pickles – and I mean a lot of them.

Seaman's Beef Balls

Perhaps the humble potato isn't as trendy as noodles from Seoul or pasta from Piedmont, but meatballs and potatoes are a perfect pairing – and this is real home cooking. Grinding the fresh bay leaves might seem like a faff, but worth the effort for the unmatched flavour.

The name comes from a classic sailor's dish, which was cooked on board a boat, and there was usually more beer on board than fresh water, hence the beer in this recipe. In this version I have replaced the meat with some lovely meatballs.

Serves 4–6; makes about 38 balls

1kg coarsely ground beef mince
1 tablespoon sea salt
1 egg, beaten
6 fresh bay leaves, ground to
   a powder in a spice grander
½ nutmeg, finely grated
freshly grated white pepper
100ml whipping cream
1 tablespoon finely shredded
   flat-leaf parsley, to garnish

For the potatoes
100g butter, for frying
400g onions, cut into 2cm-thick
   slices
1.5kg floury potatoes, peeled,
   boiled until cooked but firm
   and cut into 1cm-thick slices
375ml your favourite porter beer
about 1.2 litres beef stock

1   Beat the mince with the salt, egg, ground bay leaves, nutmeg and white pepper until the mixture becomes firmer. Add the cream and continue beating until it is smooth, firm and well combined. Shape the mixture into about 38 smooth meatballs, each 30g and the size of a table tennis ball. Set aside while preparing the rest of the recipe.

2   Meanwhile, preheat the oven to 230°C/Fan 210°C/Gas 8.

3   To prepare the potatoes, melt the butter in a large flameproof and ovenproof serving dish or pan over a medium heat. Add the onions and fry, stirring, until they are soft and a light golden colour. Use a slotted spoon to transfer the onions to a plate, then return them to the dish, layering them with the potato slices. Pour over the beer, followed by enough beef stock to just cover the potatoes, but no more.

4   Place the dish on the hob over a medium-high heat. When the stock begins to boil at the edges of the dish, it's time to put the meatballs on top of the potatoes. Transfer the dish to the oven and roast for about 15 minutes until the meatballs are cooked through when you cut one open. The liquid will be absorbed into the potatoes: it won't be completely absorbed, but this dish is not a soup.

5   I serve this at the table, still bubbling from the oven, family-style, sprinkled with the parsley. Serve in deep plates with a couple of nice pickles alongside.

Dry-aged Beef balls

served on oak planks

Here's a recipe that takes more time and effort than most, but it's ideal for a dinner party. Using roasted oak or cedar planks as serving platters is an ingenious way to add a warm, lightly smoked flavour to the meatballs, lifting them one step further. Using dry-aged meat also adds extra flavour to these meatballs, and because of the quality of the meat, you can serve them rare in the middle, rather than cooking them right through. If you don't have any suitable wooden planks, ideally cedar or oak, there are plenty available from online suppliers.

If you have any leftover meatballs, they are equally good the next day. At the restaurant we offer them as a combo with a pint, which then often turns into the start of another fun evening.

My twist on a classic duchess potato recipe is to use white pepper. It's important to use freshly ground white pepper from Indonesia, Muntok pepper, which you can source from online suppliers.

I'm overjoyed with the simple garlic butter in this recipe, which is the perfect partner for the meatballs. In the photograph I show a healthy amount on the edge of the plank.

Serves 6; makes about 36 balls

1kg dry-aged entrecôte steak or
    boneless rib-eye steak, minced
4 teaspoons sea salt
1 egg
150g red onion, finely chopped
butter, for frying
Barolo Wine Sauce (page 20),
    to serve

1. For the full impact of this recipe, you need 6 cedar or oak grilling planks that will fit in your oven.

2. Make the wine sauce (see page 20 for instructions), and set aside. For the garlic butter, whisk the butter with the garlic until light and airy. Set aside.

3. Beat the entrecôte mince with the salt and egg in a large bowl, using a wooden spoon, until the mixture becomes firmer. Add the red onion and continue beating until the mixture is smooth, firm and well combined. Shape the mixture into about 36 smooth meatballs, each 30g and the size of a table tennis ball. Set aside.

Ingredients and method continued on page 54

For the garlic butter
200g salted butter, at room
    temperature
2 garlic cloves, crushed

For the duchess potatoes
1kg floury potatoes, peeled
4 egg yolks
about 50g butter
sea salt and freshly ground
    white Muntok pepper

Classic green beans with bacon
400g green beans, trimmed
6 bacon rashers

4 To prepare the duchess potatoes, boil the potatoes in a large saucepan of salted water; the potatoes should be cooked through, but not falling apart. Drain well, then let them steam dry in the pan until they are really dry. Pass the potatoes through a potato ricer into a large bowl, or use a hand masher. Beat in the egg yolks and half of the butter, and season with salt and white pepper. Continue beating, then add the remaining butter if the mixture feels too firm. It's important to mix these ingredients together while the potatoes are still warm. Fill a piping bag, fitted with a large star nozzle, with the potatoes and pipe beautiful swirls on a serving plank for each diner.

5 Meanwhile, preheat the oven to 200°C/Fan 180°C/Gas 6.

6 Quickly prepare the green beans. Rinse the green beans in cold water, but do not dry. Lay out the bacon rashers on a large chopping board. Equally distribute the still-wet green beans on the rashers, then roll the bacon round each bundle. Transfer the bundles to the planks with the join of each underneath.

7 Roast the piped potatoes and green beans for about 15 minutes, until the bacon around the green beans is crisp, the green beans are tender and potatoes are tinged golden brown.

8 Fry the meatballs while the vegetables are in the oven. Melt enough butter in a large frying pan over a medium heat to come about one-third of the way up the meatballs. Add as many meatballs as will fit, without overcrowding, and fry, turning frequently, for about 5 minutes until brown on the outside and cooked through when you cut one open. Pan-fry in batches, if necessary. As each batch is fried transfer it to a baking tray and keep hot.

9 Reheat the wine sauce just before serving. Remove the planks from the oven and add a spoonful of the wine sauce and a portion of meatballs. Serve with a little garlic butter on the side of each and the remaining sauce in a warmed jug on the table for everyone to help themselves.

Veal and Black Garlic Balls

with pasta and marrowbone sauce

Black garlic is like candy for adults, and beef marrow gives an amazing character of meat to the pasta dish that accompanies these veal balls. A favourite of mine among ready-made sauces is HP sauce, which combines spiciness with a lovely sweetness – it's a perfect accompaniment here.

The amount of marrowbones you need to buy naturally depends on how many people you are cooking for, so allow 250g per diner.

Making your own black garlic is not difficult, but takes a long time, roasting the cloves at 65°C/149°F for at least 48 hours, but preferably more than 100 hours. Obviously, it's easier to buy.

Serves 4–6; makes about 34 balls

800g veal mince, the highest fat content you can find
1 egg, beaten
1 tablespoon sea salt
300ml whipping cream
4 black garlic cloves, grated
2 tablespoons finely chopped curly parsley
freshly ground black pepper
butter, for frying
HP Sauce, to serve, optional

1 Preheat the oven to 220°C/Fan 200°C/Gas 7, and bring a large saucepan of salted water to the boil.

2 To make the veal balls, beat the mince with the egg and salt in a large mixing bowl with a wooden spoon until the mixture becomes firmer. Add the cream, black garlic and parsley, season with black pepper, then continue beating until the mixture is smooth, firm and well combined. Shape the mixture into about 34 smooth meatballs, each 30g and the size of a table tennis ball. Set aside.

3 Season the marrowbones with salt and pepper, stand them upright in a roasting tin and roast for 15–20 minutes until the marrow is starting to bubble around the edges and is no longer pink.

4 While the bones are roasting, cook the pasta and fry the veal balls. Add the pasta to a pan of salted boiling water and boil until tender, according to the packet instructions.

Ingredients and method continued on page 57

For the pasta and marrowbone sauce

1–1.5kg beef marrowbones (see intro, above), cut into pieces 5 – 7.5 cm long and a similar diameter

450g pasta, such as trofie

60ml whipping cream

salt and freshly ground white pepper

1 tablespoon sliced black garlic, to garnish

1 tablespoon chopped curly parsley, to garnish

5 Meanwhile, melt enough butter in a large frying pan over a medium heat to come about one-third of the way up the veal balls. Add as many meatballs as will fit, without overcrowding, and fry, turning frequently, for about 7 minutes until brown on the outside and cooked through when you cut one open. Pan-fry in batches, if necessary. As each batch is fried, use a slotted spoon to transfer it to a baking tray and keep hot.

6 When the pasta cooked, drain it well, then return it to the pan over a medium heat. Add the cream and the melted marrow fat from the roasting tin with the marrowbones, and heat through. Season with salt and white pepper.

7 This is great served family-style, on a platter that everyone can help themselves from, otherwise you can serve the pasta in individual bowls, making sure there is a marrow 'cup' for everyone. (I recommend serving with a small spoon for each guest so they can pillage the marrow.) Sprinkle with black garlic and parsley and serve with the veal balls alongside, and with a bottle of HP sauce on the table, if you like.

The Seniors

with a taste of pickled herring

We specifically make these veal meatballs, with a hint of spiced pickled herring, for all the lovely pensioners who visit us at Meatballs for the People. I sometimes think of the older gentleman who comes all the way from the other side of Stockholm, sent by his wife to buy a packet of these meatballs; it warms my heart.

Serves 4–6; makes about 34 balls

200ml whipping cream
100g medium oatmeal
50g Swedish pickled herring, mashed (see tip on page 60)
1kg veal mince, with the highest fat content you can buy
1 egg, beaten
sea salt, optional
butter, for frying

For the cream sauce – the traditional sauce for meatballs

1 litre whipping cream
400ml ox broth, made by boiling a whole oxtail, or beef stock
20g Swedish pickled herring (see tip on page 60)
1 tablespoon lingonberry juice, or other unsweetened sour-tasting juice, such as cranberry or lemon

1 To make the veal balls, first mix the cream with the oatmeal. Beat in the pickled herring, then leave in the fridge for 1 hour, or until thickened.

2 To prepare the cream sauce, put the cream and ox broth in a saucepan over a medium heat and simmer, uncovered, for 30 minutes, or until reduced slightly. Add the herring, lingonberry juice and cheese, and season with white pepper. Use a stick blender to blend the sauce until it is smooth. Season with a little salt, and finish by thickening to your taste by slowly stirring in the cornflour mixture. Gently bring to the boil, stirring constantly, until the sauce is thick enough to coat the back of the spoon. You have to boil the cornflour, otherwise you will be eating raw starch. Remove from the heat, cover and keep hot.

3 To make the meatballs, beat the minced veal with the egg in a large mixing bowl with a wooden spoon until firmer. Season with salt, remembering that the pickled herring will be salty. Beat in the oatmeal mixture, then continue beating until the mixture is smooth, firm and well combined. Transfer to the fridge for a further 1 hour.

4 Shape the mixture into about 34 smooth meatballs, each 40g and the size of a golf ball.

5 Melt enough butter in a large frying pan over a medium heat to come about one-third of the way up the meatballs. Add as many meatballs as

Ingredients and method continued on page 60

1 small piece of blue cheese, such
as Stilton
2 tablespoons cornflour mixed
to a smooth paste with 1½
tablespoons water
sea salt and freshly ground
white pepper

To serve
Swedish Mashed Potatoes
(page 20)
pickled cucumbers (pages 119
and 120)
Grandpa's Lingonberries
(page 116; optional)

will fit, without overcrowding, and fry, turning frequently, for about
10 minutes until brown on the outside and cooked through when you
cut one open. Pan-fry in batches, if necessary. As each batch is fried
use a slotted spoon to transfer it to a tray and keep hot.

6 Just before serving, reheat the sauce, if necessary. Put all the meatballs
in a beautiful warmed serving bowl or on a platter and serve with the
classic accompaniments – mashed potatoes, cream sauce and pickled
cucumbers. Lingonberries are good, too.

MATHIAS' TIP: Pickled Herring Spice Mix

If you cannot get hold of pickled herring, here's a clever hack to capture the
quintessential Swedish flavour. There are many recipes, but here is mine, and
I'm more than happy to share. Several of these spices are strong in flavour,
but basically you need an equal weight of each ingredient. This will keep in
a sealed air-tight container in a dark place for up to three months.

Makes 7 tablespoons

8 dried bay leaves
3 star anise
4cm piece cinnamon stick
4g cloves
4g dried ginger
4g black peppercorns
2 tablespoons dried oregano
2½ teaspoons red sandalwood
powder
2 teaspoons green cardamom
powder
1½ teaspoons nigella seeds

1 Mix all the ingredients in a spice or
coffee grinder until really well ground.

2 For the veal balls, add 1 tablespoon
of this spice mixture to the mince in
place of the pickled herring, then taste
and add more mixture, if you want.

3 To use in the cream sauce, add 1½
teaspoons to the sauce in place of the
pickled herring.

Viggo's Chicken and Squid Balls

This recipe is quite new to our menu. I am fond of squid in all its forms, so, of course I wanted to produce a recipe for a ball incorporating squid. I tested this recipe on my youngest son, Viggo, who gave it his seal of approval, so that is how the recipe came to be known as Viggo's Chicken and Squid Balls. When you're entertaining, you can cook the balls and assemble the skewers in advance, ready for reheating just before serving.

Makes about 28 balls

200g gutted squid, the grey membrane removed and the flesh finely chopped, with the tentacles reserved
sesame oil, for frying the tentacles
1 teaspoon crushed garlic
800g boneless chicken breasts and thighs, minced
2 teaspoons sea salt
150ml whipping cream
sunflower oil, for frying the balls
fresh mint, to garnish
3 limes, thinly sliced, plus extra wedges, for serving
sriracha chilli sauce, to serve
steamed jasmine rice, to serve

1 At least an hour before you plan to make the balls, rub the tentacles with sesame oil, so they are just coated. Heat a large, dry, ideally nonstick, frying pan over a high heat. Add the tentacles and stir-fry for 30 seconds, or until they curl and develop a reddish hue. Remove from the pan and set aside. When cool enough to handle, cut in half or quarter.

2 Wipe out the pan and return it to the heat, without any oil. Add the chopped squid and stir-fry for 30 seconds. Add the garlic and continue stir-frying for a further 30 seconds, or until the squid turns white and becomes firmer. Watch the garlic closely so it does not burn. This step is to remove the liquid from the squid and for the garlic to take on a softer taste. Remove both from the pan and leave to cool completely, then chill in the fridge for at least an hour. (The secret to good meatballs is to have all your ingredients as cold as possible.)

3 Just before you are ready to cook, preheat the oven to 200°C/Fan 180°C/Gas 6.

4 Beat the chicken mince with the salt in a large mixing bowl with a wooden spoon until it becomes firmer. Beat in the cream and the chopped squid and continue beating until the mixture is smooth, firm and well combined, with the squid evenly distributed throughout. With dampened hands, shape the mixture into about 28 fairly smooth balls, 30g each and the size of a table tennis ball.

Continued on page 63

5 Heat a 1cm layer of sunflower oil in a large frying pan over a medium heat. Add as many balls as will fit, without overcrowding, and fry, turning frequently, until lightly browned all over and cooked in the middle when you cut one open. Be careful not to break them up while turning them. Pan-fry in batches, if necessary. As each batch is fried, use a slotted spoon to remove from the pan and set aside.

6 To assemble the skewers, thread the balls, squid tentacles, fresh mint leaves and lime slices on to wooden skewers.

7 Place the skewers on an ovenproof platter and transfer to the oven for 10 minutes until the meatballs are just hot. Serve with sriracha or another sauce full of Asian flavours and with jasmine rice and lime wedges on the side.

Pikeballs with Tomatoes in Dill Cream

Pike, a freshwater fish, is fun to fish, but difficult to cook because of the large number of bones. However, it is absolutely fantastic to make mince out of, and tastes super delicious. Here, I've used dill oil to drizzle over just before serving, for extra flavour. If blood oranges aren't in season, substitute with pink grapefruit.

Serves 4–6; makes about 28 balls

700g skinned and boned pike, very finely minced
4 teaspoons sea salt
200ml whipping cream
1 tablespoon grated blood orange zest
2 teaspoons dill seeds, finely ground
butter, for frying
dill oil, to serve
boiled new potatoes, halved, to serve, optional

For the tomatoes in dill cream
600ml whipping cream
freshly grated nutmeg
sea salt and freshly ground white pepper
10 tomatoes in assorted colours, cut in different shapes
4 dill crowns, or fresh dill sprigs, finely chopped, plus extra to garnish
2 blood oranges, cut into wedges, to serve

1 Beat the minced pike with the salt in a large mixing bowl with a wooden spoon until it becomes firmer. Add the cream, blood orange zest and ground dill seeds, and continue beating until the mixture is smooth, firm and well combined. With dampened hands, shape into about 28 smooth balls, each 30g and the size of a table tennis ball.

2 Melt enough butter to make a 2cm layer in a large frying pan over a medium heat. You want enough butter so the meatballs are bathed in foaming butter while they cook. Add as many meatballs as will fit, without overcrowding, and fry, turning frequently, for about 5 minutes until they are lightly browned all over, crisp and cooked through when you cut one open. Pan-fry in batches, if necessary. As each batch is fried, use a slotted spoon to transfer it to a baking tray and keep hot.

3 Meanwhile, prepare the tomatoes. Pour the cream into a saucepan, season with nutmeg, salt and white pepper, and bring to the boil. Reduce the heat and simmer for 5 minutes. Add the tomatoes and continue simmering until they are just warm, but not soft. Finish by adding the chopped dill and a squeeze of blood orange juice. Adjust the seasoning, if necessary.

4 Serve the pike balls on warmed plates with the tomatoes and sauce. Drizzle with dill oil and serve a few wedges of blood orange alongside for squeezing over. You want to make sure this dish has a definite dill flavour, so sprinkle over extra dill to serve. Serve with boiled potatoes, if you wish.

Coconut Balls

never forget a sweet ball

 After traditional meatballs, these must be the most famous balls in Sweden! We at Meatballs for the People have a lot of different variations, as all of us who work here know someone who claims to have the best recipe, and this is mine. After you've scraped the seeds from the vanilla pod, pop the pod in a sealed jar of caster sugar and leave indefinitely to flavour the sugar.

Makes about 24 balls

1kg medium oatmeal
250g icing sugar
1 vanilla pod, split lengthwise
   and seeds scraped out with
   the pod reserved
125g unsweetened cocoa
   powder – use a good-quality
   brand, such as Valrhona
50ml whipping cream
50ml Licor 43 or Galliano
500g butter, at room
   temperature and whipped
   until light and airy
200g desiccated coconut,
   to decorate

1   Using a large metal spoon, mix the oatmeal, icing sugar, vanilla seeds and cocoa powder together in a large mixing. Add the cream and Licor 43 and continue mixing until all the ingredients are blended. Add the whipped butter and beat until everything is well combined. It's important, however, that the oatmeal does not get too processed and still retains texture.

2   Shape the mixture into about 24 smooth balls, 40g each and the size of a golf ball.

3   Spread the coconut over a tray and roll the balls, one at a time, in the coconut to thoroughly coat. You want to make sure there's enough coconut on them that they become difficult to eat, with coconut raining on to your shirt. I serve these at room temperature. If not serving immediately, however, store in an air-tight container in the fridge for up to 2 weeks and remove 30 minutes before serving.

Ch. 4   Meatballs Around the World

Tenderloin Meatballs

with flavours from Provence

For this dish I use the tail and head of the beef tenderloin, pieces that are not as sought after as other cuts of the cow, but that make luxury meatballs once the meat is ground. These particular meatballs are also good served with beef gravy or Barolo Wine Sauce (page 20).

The magnificent Tore Wretman, the godfather of Swedish cuisine, was heavily inspired by his time in southern France, and he was a big fan of Provençal flavours, especially garlic. This recipe is my homage to him.

Serves 4–6; makes about 34 balls

1kg beef tenderloin, minced
1 tablespoon Dijon mustard
1 tablespoon celery salt
freshly ground white pepper
sunflower oil, for frying

For the garlic butter
250g butter, room temperature
3 garlic cloves, crushed – you
    can add more or use less,
    depending on your preference
1 teaspoon sea salt, optional
25g natural or Greek yogurt

1 First prepare the garlic butter. Whisk the butter with the garlic and salt (if using) until it's light and airy. Add the yogurt and continue whisking until smooth. Using clingfilm or parchment paper to help roll the butter, shape it into a log about 4cm thick, twisting the ends. Wrap again in clingfilm and transfer to the freezer, for at least 1 hour or up to about 3 months.

2 Beat the minced beef, mustard, celery salt and white pepper together in a large mixing bowl with a wooden spoon until the mixture becomes smooth, firm and well combined. You can taste this mince raw to check that you are happy with the seasoning. (And it's super tasty eaten on a salty biscuit.) Shape the mixture into about 34 smooth meatballs, each 30g and the size of a table tennis ball, rolling them quite firmly to compress, otherwise they'll break when you fry them. Set aside.

3 To cook the potatoes, heat a 0.5cm layer of oil in a large frying pan over a medium-high heat. Add the potato slices, shaking the pan thoroughly at the beginning, so all the slices get evenly coated in oil. Fry for about 15 minutes, stirring occasionally, until the potatoes start to colour on both sides. Lower the heat, add a little butter, season with chilli flakes

Ingredients and method continued on page 72

For the fried potatoes with raw mushrooms

sunflower oil, for frying

1kg new or other waxy potatoes, cut into 1cm-thick slices

butter, for frying

½ teaspoon red chilli flakes

sea salt and freshly ground white pepper

1 tablespoon finely chopped curly parsley

10 very fresh brown mushrooms, thinly sliced

and salt and pepper, and turn the potatoes over. The aroma should now smell lovely from the browned butter and the potatoes should be crispy. Set aside and keep warm on the hob until the meatballs are fried and you're ready to serve.

4 Meanwhile, heat a thin layer of oil that just covers the surface of a large frying pan over a medium-high heat. Add as many balls as will fit, without overcrowding, and fry for about 3 minutes, shaking the pan and turning frequently, until browned on the outside. It's important they get warm in the centre, but they don't need to be cooked through when you cut one open. Pan-fry in batches, if necessary. As each batch is fried, use a slotted spoon to transfer it to a warmed serving platter, so your friends or family get two helpings of freshly fried tenderloin meatballs.

5 To serve, use a slotted spoon to remove the potatoes from the pan, shaking to remove excess butter and oil, and transfer to the platter. Garnish with parsley and add the sliced mushrooms to the platter – their rawness gives a little extra freshness. Add the meatballs to the platter and coarsely grate over a generous serving of the frozen garlic butter.

Veal Balls

stuffed with Karl Johan mushrooms

This recipe takes its inspiration from the cuisine of northern Italy. Just like the Italians, we Swedes love the porcini mushroom. Here in Sweden, however, the porcini is named after our French-born King Karl XIV Johan Bernadotte (1763–1844), who taught us poor farmers to appreciate porcini. Thank you, Sir!

The meatballs go really well with many accompaniments, and for the photo I've chosen a creamy risotto with loads of Parmesan cheese, and extra fried porcini to serve alongside – and a good, rich Barolo wine sauce (page 20).

Makes 20 balls

1kg veal mince, with at least
   12% fat content
1 tablespoon sea salt
2 eggs
200ml whipping cream
butter, for frying

For the mushroom stuffing
50g butter
300g Karl Johan mushrooms
   (fresh porcini), trimmed and
   finely chopped, or 60g dried
   porcini, soaked in warm water
   for 30 minutes, drained
100g shallots, finely chopped
100ml whipping cream
2 tablespoons finely shredded
   basil
sea salt and freshly ground
   black pepper

1 Before you start this recipe make sure you have enough ice-cube trays and freezer space to freeze 20 portions of the mushroom stuffing. If you have round ice-cube moulds, all the better.

2 First make the stuffing. Melt the butter in a large frying pan over a medium heat. Add the mushrooms and fry for 5 minutes, stirring. Add the shallots and continue frying until the shallots are golden brown. Stir in the cream and continue stirring until the pan is almost dry. The mushrooms should be nice and creamy. Season with basil, salt and a couple of turns of a peppermill. Divide the mixture among 20 ice-cube tray segments and leave to cool, then freeze for at least 2 hours.

3 To make the veal balls, use a wooden spoon to beat the mince with the salt and eggs in a large mixing bowl until the mixture becomes firmer. Add the cream and continue beating until the mixture is smooth, firm and well combined. It's important that the mince is not too soft, because we will be putting the mushroom stuffing in the middle of the meatballs. Divide into 20 equal portions, about 55g each.

Continued on page 75

4 Remove the mushroom stuffing from the freezer and pop each portion out of the ice-cube tray. Put one portion of stuffing in the centre of each meatball, then mould the mince mixture around the stuffing until it entirely enclosed. Repeat until all the mince mixture and stuffing portions are used. When all the meatballs are stuffed and shaped, set them aside at room temperature for 30 minutes so they are not still frozen in the centre when you cook them.

5 When you are ready to cook, melt enough butter in a large frying pan over a medium heat to come about one-third of the way up the meatballs. Add as many meatballs as will fit, without overcrowding and fry, turning frequently, for 15–20 minutes until brown on the outside and cooked through when you cut one open. Pan-fry in batches, if necessary. As each batch is fried, use a slotted spoon to transfer the meatballs to a baking tray and keep hot.

6 These meatballs are best served directly from the frying pan or baking tray, with the accompaniments of your choice.

Chinese Pork Balls

on lemongrass skewers

Using a lemongrass stalk as a skewer is a great trick that imparts extra flavour to these Asian-inspired balls, and also makes the presentation interesting. Sometimes we light a barbecue outside the restaurant just to cook the pork balls, encouraging our neighbours to join us. Alternatively, you can cook these under a preheated medium-high grill.

Makes about 38 balls

1kg pork mince
1 tablespoon sea salt
100ml iced water
1 garlic clove, crushed
lemongrass stalks, with outer
   layer removed, as skewers

For the spice mix; makes 1½
   tablespoons
1 teaspoon coriander seeds
¾ teaspoon cloves
¾ teaspoon Szechuan (Sichuan)
   peppercorns
½ teaspoon dill seeds
½ teaspoon fennel seeds
½ teaspoon black peppercorns
2g piece cinnamon stick

1 First make the spice mix. Put all the ingredients in a spice grinder, or use a pestle and mortar, and grind until you have a fine powder. Store what you don't use immediately in a well-sealed container in a dark place for up to 3 months.

2 To make the pork balls, beat the mince with the salt in a large mixing bowl with a wooden spoon until it is firmer. Add the water, garlic and 1 teaspoon of the spice mix, and continue beating until the mixture is smooth, firm and well combined. Shape the mixture into about 38 smooth balls, each 30g and the size of a table tennis ball. Thread these on to lemongrass skewers, shaping the mixture around the skewers to make sure they're well stuck on. Place in the fridge until you're ready to cook.

3 Before you're ready to cook, preheat your barbecue. When the coals are glowing, place the skewers on the cooking rack. Because these meatballs contain a lot of fat, they are likely to smoke and flame a bit, so be careful. Make sure the meatballs are well grilled on one side before turning, otherwise they might break apart. The actual cooking time will depend on the heat of your barbecue, but I usually cook these for about 10 minutes before serving. Cut one open to make sure they are cooked through. If you are cooking in batches, transfer to a baking tray and keep hot on the side of the barbecue or in a preheated oven.

Thai-style Pork and Prawn Balls

 Who doesn't love the Thai food culture, with its incredible flavours and taste of street markets? This is my meatball take on traditional Thai street food.

Serves 6; makes about 50 balls

700g pork mince
300g prawns, shelled, deveined
   and chopped, with 6 heads
   reserved
1 tablespoon sea salt
2 tablespoons finely chopped
   fresh coriander
1 tablespoon freshly grated
   galangal
sunflower oil, for frying

*For the jasmine rice with crispy
   prawn heads*
250g jasmine rice
sunflower oil, for frying
6 prawn heads (reserved from
   the prawns above)
Thai fish sauce (this has a strong
   flavour so add a little to start
   with; I like it strong, but use as
   much as suits your taste)

To garnish
shiso cress leaves
prawn crisps
sesame seeds

1   Beat the pork mince, prawn meat and salt in a large mixing bowl with a wooden spoon until the mixture becomes firmer. Add the coriander and galangal and continue beating until the mixture is smooth, firm and well combined. I make these into fairly small meatballs, so shape the mixture into about 50 smooth balls, each 20g and the size of a walnut. You can make these in advance and keep in the fridge until you're ready to cook.

2   Meanwhile, cook the rice for the jasmine rice and crispy prawn heads, according to the instructions on the packet. Drain well and set aside.

3   To cook the pork and prawn balls, heat enough sunflower oil to cover the bottom of a large frying pan over a medium-high heat. Add as many meatballs as will fit, without overcrowding, and fry for about 5 minutes until they take on an amber colour. It's important to shake the pan and keep the balls moving while they are frying. The prawns in the balls can release a little liquid so if they start to spit, they are beginning to overcook. Pan-fry in batches, if necessary. As each batch is fried, use a slotted spoon to transfer it to a baking tray and keep hot.

4   Meanwhile, finish the rice. Heat a thin layer of oil in a separate frying pan over a medium heat. Add the prawn heads and stir-fry until they turn red/orange in colour. Add the cooked rice, lower the heat and stir-fry for a few minutes until the rice is hot and takes on the flavour of the prawn heads. Add the fish sauce to taste, taking care as it can sputter when it hits the hot oil.

5   To serve, arrange the shiso cress on your serving plates, then add a hearty spoonful of the rice, making sure everyone gets a fried prawn head. Top with the pork and prawn balls and prawn crisps, and sprinkle with sesame seeds.

North African-style Lamb Balls
with spiced tomato salad

 Lamb balls are always on our menu. Because of lamb's strong taste, I pair it with other full-flavoured ingredients, such as ras el hanout. I mix the lamb balls with the salad when serving, with couscous on the side.

Serves 4–6; makes about 36 balls

1kg lamb mince
1 egg
100ml chicken stock, chilled
1 tablespoon ras el hanout
3 tablespoons finely chopped
  flat-leaf parsley
butter, for frying
cooked couscous, to serve
sea salt

For the spiced tomato salad
500g tomatoes, roughly chopped
2 avocados, cut into thin wedges
2 celery sticks, finely sliced
2 green peppers pieces, roughly
  chopped
1 red onion, cut into wedges
½ cucumber, roughly chopped
100ml virgin olive oil
300ml Bloody Mary mix or
  tomato or vegetable juice
green Tabasco sauce
1 tablespoon each roughly
  shredded fresh coriander
  and mint

1 First prepare the salad. Put all the vegetables in a bowl. Whisk the olive oil and Bloody Mary mix together, then stir it through the vegetables. Season with a couple splashes of green Tabasco sauce and salt to taste, then scatter over the coriander and mint. Transfer to a large platter and set aside to let all the flavours blend – you want to serve this at room temperature.

2 To make the lamb balls, beat the lamb mince, egg and 2 teaspoons of salt together in a large mixing bowl with a wooden spoon until the mixture becomes firmer. Add the chicken stock, ras el hanout and parsley, and continue beating until the mixture is smooth, firm and well combined. Shape the mixture into about 36 smooth meatballs, each 30g and the size of a table tennis ball.

3 Melt enough butter in a large frying pan over a medium heat to come about one-third of the way up the meatballs. Add as many meatballs as will fit, without overcrowding, and fry, turning frequently, for 7–10 minutes until brown on the outside and cooked through when you cut one open. Pan-fry in batches, if necessary. As each batch is fried, transfer it to a baking tray and keep hot.

4 To serve, transfer the meatballs and salad to a serving platter. Serve with couscous on the side, if you wish.

Rooter and the Lobster

 I often serve these Mexican-inspired balls bathed in a rich, creamy sauce, with crisp, golden French fries.

Makes about 38 balls

700g boneless, skinless chicken
 breasts and thighs, minced
2 teaspoons sea salt
200ml whipping cream
I teaspoon coriander seeds
I tablespoon finely chopped
 seeded jalapeño chilli
2 cooked lobsters, each weighing
 at least 400g, the meat
 removed and chopped, with
 the shells saved for the sauce
butter, for frying
pickled cucumber, to serve

*For the world's fastest lobster
 sauce*
lobster shells from I lobster,
 roughly crushed
I litre whipping cream
100g pecorino cheese, finely
 grated
2 tablespoons virgin olive oil

1   Beat the chicken mince with the salt in a large mixing bowl with a wooden spoon until it becomes firmer. Add the cream, spices and lobster meat, and continue beating until the mixture is smooth, firm and well combined. Leave the mixture to rest in the fridge for at least 30 minutes.

2   While the mince mixture is resting, make the sauce. Put the lobster shells in a large saucepan, along with any liquid from the shells, as there's lots of flavour in that liquid. Add the cream and bring to the boil, then reduce the heat and simmer for 5 minutes. Turn off the heat and leave the mixture to stand, uncovered, for 20 minutes for the flavours to blend. Sieve the cream into a blender (discard the lobster shells), add the pecorino and blend until smooth. Finish by blending in the olive oil. Reheat gently and whisk with a balloon whisk just before serving.

3   With dampened hands, shape the chicken and lobster mixture into about 38 smooth balls, each 30g and the size of a table tennis ball.

4   Melt enough butter in a large frying pan over a medium heat to come about one-third of the way up the balls. Add as many balls as will fit, without overcrowding, and fry, turning frequently, for about 10 minutes until brown on the outside and cooked through when you cut one open. Pan-fry in batches, if necessary. As each batch is fried, use a slotted spoon transfer it to a baking tray and keep hot.

5   To serve, fill each plate with the balls, the foamy sauce and some pickled cucumber, which cuts through the richness of the sauce.

Lime and Chipotle Rabbit Balls

with polenta tamales

 This is my take on tamales, one of my favourite Mexican dishes, but here it's all about a fun presentation. I've chosen to make these spicy balls with rabbit, a lean meat that needs something creamy as an accompaniment, hence the polenta filling for the tamales.

Serves 5; makes about 40 balls

1kg boneless rabbit meat, minced
1 egg
1 tablespoon sea salt
200ml whipping cream
1 tablespoon freshly grated
   lime zest
1 teaspoon chipotle chilli powder
½ teaspoon ground allspice
butter, for frying

For the polenta tamales
5 corn cobs, with the husks saved
   for serving
1 litre chicken stock, made from
   a roasted chicken carcass
300g fine polenta
100g butter, diced
200g Parmesan cheese, freshly
   grated, plus extra, to garnish
dried red chilli flakes, to garnish

1   Preheat the oven to 200°C/Fan 180°C/Gas 6.

2   First prepare the corn cobs for the polenta tamales. Partially peel the cobs, remove and discard the corn silk and replace the husks, then put the cobs, in their husks, directly on the oven shelf and roast for 30–35 minutes until tender.

3   Meanwhile, make the rabbit balls. Beat the rabbit mince with the egg and salt in a large mixing bowl until the mixture becomes firmer. Add the cream, lime zest, chilli powder and ground allspice, and continue beating the mixture until it becomes smooth, firm and well combined. Shape the mixture into about 40 smooth balls, each 30g and the size of a table tennis ball. Set aside.

4   When the corn cobs are cooked, remove them from the oven and reduce the oven temperature to 170°C/Fan 150°C/Gas 3. Set aside the cobs until they are cool enough to handle, then remove the husks and slice off the kernels. Tear a thin strip of husk off each, which will be used to tie the ends of the husks. Set everything aside separately.

5   To make the polenta tamales, first make the polenta. Bring the chicken stock to the boil in a large saucepan. Add the polenta in a fine stream, whisking until it thickens and is smooth. Continue whisking over a low heat for 1 minute. Add the butter to the thickened polenta and stir over

Continued on page 86

a low heat until it melts, then stir in the Parmesan; the polenta should be creamy. If it is too thick, dilute with a little water. Season with the salt to taste. Add half of the corn kernels and give it a good stir.

6   Put the corn husks on a baking tray and divide the polenta among them, then use the thin strips of husk to tie a small knot at one end of each, so they hold a nice shape. Sprinkle with the remaining corn kernels and heat them through in the oven.

7   Meanwhile, fry the meatballs. Melt enough butter to come about one-third of the way up the meatballs in a large frying pan over a medium heat. Add as many balls as will fit, without overcrowding, and fry for about 10 minutes, turning often, until crisp on the outside and cooked in the middle when you cut one open. Be careful not to break them up while stirring. Pan-fry in batches, if necessary. As each batch is fried, use a slotted spoon to transfer it to a baking tray and keep hot.

8   I serve the polenta tamales in the baking tray, sprinkling with more Parmesan cheese and a few chilli flakes, along with the meatballs and a nice cold beer or two. A cake slice is particularly useful for serving the tamales.

Chickpea Balls with Hummus

One day I will open my own falafel bar. We don't have many veggie recipes at MFTP, but this is one of my favourites, inspired by my many visits to Falafelbaren, an excellent falafel bar on Hornsgatan, near where I live in Stockholm. They are well worth a visit if you're in the city.

Serves 4–6; makes about 40 balls, depending on the size

1kg dried chickpeas
2 large onions, roughly chopped
2 garlic cloves, peeled
2 green chillies, roughly chopped
    with seeds left in
4 tablespoons shredded flat-leaf
    parsley
3 tablespoons shredded fresh
    coriander
2 tablespoons shredded fresh
    mint
2 tablespoons ground cumin
1 teaspoon smoked paprika
2 teaspoons sea salt
1 teaspoon bicarbonate of soda
100g shelled smoked almonds,
    coarsely crushed
vegetable oil, for deep-frying
watercress sprigs, rinsed and
    dried, to garnish

For the hummus
300g cooked chickpeas, drained
    and rinsed, especially if tinned
2 garlic cloves, crushed
2 teaspoons sea salt

1   The day before making the chickpea balls, put the dried chickpeas in a large bowl of water to cover and leave to soak for 24 hours. The next day, drain well and set aside until ready to make the balls.

2   On the day you are cooking, first make the hummus. Put the cooked and drained (or tinned) chickpeas, garlic, salt and lemon juice in a food processor, and blitz until smooth. Add the tahini and olive oil and mix again until well blended. Add a little cold water, if necessary, until the hummus has your preferred consistency. Season with white pepper to taste. Transfer to a bowl and set aside until ready to serve.

3   To make the chickpea balls, put the onions, garlic, chillies, herbs, spices, salt and bicarbonate of soda together into a food processor, and blend until the mixture is almost smooth. Add the soaked and drained chickpeas and continue to blend until the mixture has a rough consistency; it is important that the mixture isn't too smooth, or the balls won't stick together. Shape the mixture into about 40 smooth balls, each 25–30g and the size of a walnut or table tennis ball. Chill the balls in the fridge for at least 1 hour before frying.

4   Meanwhile, prepare the vegetables. Preheat the oven to 220°C/Fan 200°C/Gas 7. Put the aubergine halves in a large roasting tin and spoon over most of the olive oil. Roast for 20–25 minutes until the aubergines are tender, but not too soft. Remove the tin from the oven and leave the aubergines to cool a little; do not wash the tin.

Ingredients and method continued on page 89

4 tablespoons lemon juice
5 tablespoons tahini
100ml olive oil
freshly ground white pepper

For the vegetables
4 aubergines, halved lengthwise
300ml olive oil
2 blood oranges, halved and cut
  into wedges
300g shelled sweet green peas
1 teaspoon red chilli flakes
sea salt
100g pickled red onions

5   Once the aubergines are cool enough to handle, cut a long wedge, with the skin attached, for each serving. Peel the remaining aubergine halves and cut the flesh into cubes.

6   Put the aubergine cubes back in the roasting tin with the remaining olive oil. Squeeze over the juice from half the blood orange wedges and add the remaining blood orange wedges and the peas to the tin. Sprinkle with chilli flakes and sea salt, then finish by giving everything a good stir. Add the pickled red onions and set aside until ready to serve.

7   Just before you are ready to fry the chickpea balls, roll them gently in the crushed smoked almonds until they are lightly covered.

8   Heat enough vegetable oil for deep-frying in a deep-fat fryer or large, heavy-based saucepan to 190°C when tested on a digital thermometer (if you don't have a digital thermometer, the oil is hot enough when a small piece of the chickpea ball mixture sizzles, turns brown and quickly rises to the surface when placed in the oil).

9   Deep-fry in batches to avoid overcrowding, and make sure the temperature returns to 190°C after each batch, until the balls are dark golden brown and cooked through when you cut one open. It's important to keep the oil at this temperature, otherwise the balls will fall apart. As each batch is fried, use a slotted spoon to transfer it to a baking tray lined with greaseproof paper and keep hot. These are the absolute best when you serve them straightaway.

10 Arrange the vegetables with hearty spoonfuls of hummus in deep plates, and then add the freshly fried chickpea balls as soon as they're all cooked. Serve any extra vegetables and hummus at the table.

Turbot and Oyster Balls

Because it's so expensive, turbot tends to be a rare treat, but it's one of my favourite types of fish. I think it's nice to save the head and bones when you fillet the turbot (or ask the fishmonger for them), and then roast them in the oven or cook under a high grill to use for presentation. To finish the dish, very lightly fry some citrus fruit – I like pink grapefruit segments, but oranges work well, too – and blanch a salty sea plant such as samphire in boiling water for 2–3 minutes to serve alongside. Arrange everything on a large platter, and serve these lovely fish balls with freshly baked bread and aïoli.

Makes about 44 balls

butter, for greasing the baking tray and frying
1kg skinned turbot fillets, with 700g minced and 300g finely diced
2 teaspoons sea salt
200ml whipping cream
20 oysters, shucked and finely chopped, with the liquid from the shells reserved
1 tablespoon finely grated lemon zest

To serve

citrus fruit, such as pink grapefruit segments and orange slices, grilled
fresh samphire, well rinsed and trimmed
freshly baked rolls
aïoli

1   Preheat the oven to 200°C/Fan 180°C/Gas 6, and butter a baking tray large enough to hold all the fish balls in a single layer.

2   Beat the minced turbot with the salt in a large mixing bowl with a wooden spoon until it becomes firmer. Beat in the cream and chopped oysters, and gradually add up to 200ml of the oyster liquid, beating until the mixture is smooth, firm and well combined. Gently stir in the diced turbot and lemon zest so they are evenly distributed. With dampened hands, shape the mixture into about 44 smooth balls, each 30g and the size of a table tennis ball.

3   Put the balls on the baking tray and roast for about 15 minutes until firm; they shouldn't take on much colour at this point. The balls might have a more rustic look and no longer be perfectly round, but that's fine.

4   Melt enough butter in a large frying pan over a medium heat to come about one-third of the way up the meatballs. Add as many meatballs as will fit, without overcrowding, and fry, turning frequently, for about 10 minutes until brown on the outside. They have already cooked through in the oven, so you're just finishing them here. It's important they don't get too hot, as they can burn and stick to the pan. Pan-fry in batches, if necessary. As each batch is fried, use a slotted spoon to transfer it to a baking tray to keep hot. Serve with any of the accompaniments you like.

Ch. 5   Dinner with Friends

Sharing a meal with friends is, I think, the best way to
have dinner, and if you can arrange it in a restaurant, then
it becomes absolutely magical. You can recreate that same
pleasure at home easily enough. I recently got a bunch
of lovely friends together for a relaxed evening of good
conversation, good wine, lots of laughs and, of course,
good food, with the emphasis on – you've guessed it –
meatballs.

Here's a selection of some of the numerous morsels
I put together, but you don't have to follow this menu
exactly. For a bit of variety, I added a few small tacos
filled with *pico de gallo*, the spicy Mexican salsa, which
gives a sharp contrast to the rich meatballs. Remember,
this meal is all about the experience and quality time,
so mix and match the recipes throughout this book,
as you like. Anything goes!

Tuna, Caviar and Truffle Balls

My dinner with friends started with these no-cook snacks, while we all enjoyed pre-dinner drinks. I got inspiration for this dish after a late-night visit to a dinner club in New York City several years ago. After dinner a group of us went to the nearest bar and tasted these memorable morsels. They are a little fancy, but well worth the effort. These delicate little taste bombs can be tricky to pick up, so make sure they're spaciously arranged on plates so your guests can easily reach them.

Another recipe that's good for serving with drinks is Thai-style Pork and Prawn Balls (page 79). You can omit the rice in the recipe, or serve them on individual spoons so you get a bite of rice with each ball.

Makes about 28 balls

500g sushi-quality tuna, cut into small, fine cubes
sea salt
10g white Alba truffles, half finely grated and half thinly sliced (black truffle would work if you cannot source fresh white Alba truffles)
1 sheet nori, preferably roasted, cut into 28 1cm-wide strips
50g black caviar, to garnish

1 Beat the tuna in a large mixing bowl with a wooden spoon, then add salt to taste and continue beating until the fish becomes firmer. A few pieces of the tuna will break up, but that's fine, as it allows you to shape the tuna into small balls. Add the grated truffle and stir a few times until it is evenly distributed.

2 Shape the mixture into about 28 smooth, bite-size balls, each 20g. If the mixture is difficult to shape, then give it another stir to break it all down a bit more. Try to get a really nice round and smooth shape to your tuna balls, then wrap a strip of nori seaweed, like a belt, around each. Use a finger to lightly moisten one end of the nori strip, and secure both ends together. Top each ball with the caviar and truffle slices.

3 You can prepare the balls well in advance, but only attach the nori strips just before serving, so they are still crisp enough to give a lovely contrast to the soft tuna.

The Hipster Meatballs

I introduced these unusual veal, rabbit and lobster meatballs to the menu within a year of opening Meatballs for the People. The area of Stockholm where we are located, SOFO, is the city's most hipster area, so I wanted to produce a meatball specifically for our neighbourhood guests.

These hipster meatballs are very adaptable. If you steam them, instead of pan-frying, they are lovely served with a simple salad, but they are also delicious served with linguine topped with masses of grated pecorino. I like to add the ruby red lobster shells to the pan for serving, both for zing on the table and for guests to pick out any remaining bits of meat. Such a treat! However, if you're feeling less fancy, then you just need 200g cooked lobster meat for the meatballs.

Serves 4–6; makes about 34 balls

2 live lobsters, about 450g each
500g veal mince, minced twice
1 tablespoon sea salt
100ml whipping cream
200g boneless, grilled or cooked rabbit meat, chopped into small pieces
50g shelled pistachios, finely chopped
1 tablespoon finely sliced fresh basil, plus extra to garnish
½ fresh red chilli, deseeded and finely chopped, or 1 teaspoon red chilli flakes
butter, for frying
450g linguine

1 Before you start cooking, put the lobsters in the freezer for 2 hours, or until almost frozen – this makes them unconscious, and is the most humane way to prepare them for cooking.

2 Bring a large saucepan of salted water to the boil. Add the lobsters head first into the boiling water, holding them under with a wooden spoon. When the water returns to the boil, blanch them for 4 minutes. Use tongs to remove the lobsters from the water and run them under cold running water to stop the cooking. Do not discard the cooking water, because you will use it later for cooking the linguine.

3 When the lobsters are cool enough to handle, crack open the shells and remove the meat and finely chop. You will need 200g cooked meat for the balls, any extra can be served on the side or from the shells.

4 Beat the veal mince with the salt until firmer, then add the cream and stir around a couple of times to loosen. Beat in the rabbit meat, lobster meat, pistachios, basil and chilli, and continue beating until the mixture is

Continued on page 97

smooth, firm and well combined. It is important that all the ingredients are evenly distributed, with solid pieces of rabbit and lobster throughout the mixture, but retaining their shape. Shape the mixture into about 34 smooth meatballs, each 30g and the size of a table tennis ball.

5   Melt enough butter to come about one-third of the way up the meatballs in a large frying pan over a medium heat. Add as many balls as will fit, without overcrowding, and fry for about 10 minutes until crisp on the outside and cooked in the middle when you cut one open. Pan-fry in batches, if necessary. As each batch is cooked, use a slotted spoon to transfer it to a baking tray and keep hot. Keep the juices in the pan.

6   Meanwhile, return the lobster-cooking water to the boil. Add the linguine and boil for 10–12 minutes, or according to the packet instructions, until tender. Drain well, then immediately add the linguine to the pan you fried the balls in and toss with all the buttery juices. Add the balls and the lobster shells to the pan, scatter with basil and then serve straight from the pan for everyone to help themselves.

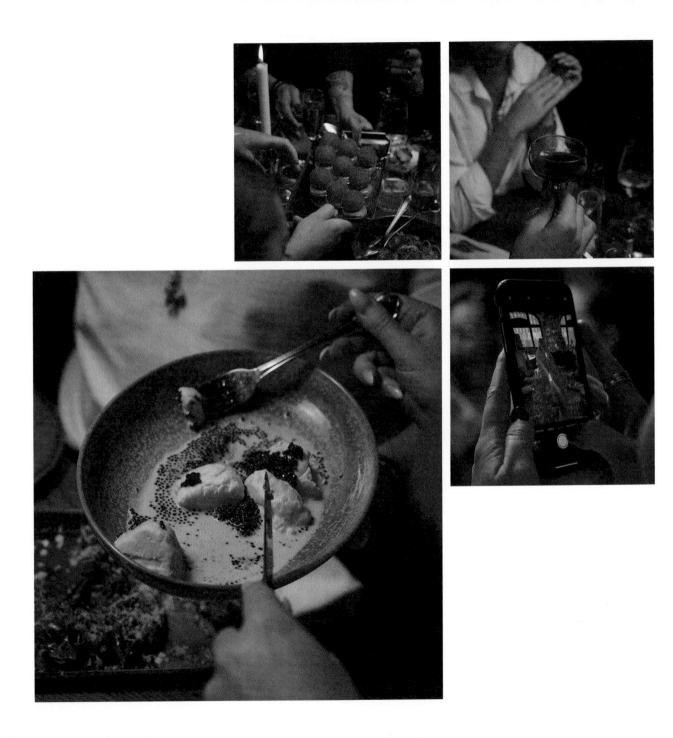

Steak Tartare Meatballs

 I think these little balls are magical, but it is incredibly important that the beef is top quality and very fresh. These meatballs are little flirt with classic tartar, and if you can get the outsides crisply fried while keeping the centres rare then you're a top chef!

Makes about 36 balls

700g beef fillet or tenderloin,
   tartare quality
50g shallots, finely chopped
20g capers, drained and finely
   chopped
1 tablespoon Dijon mustard
50g pickled red beetroot, drained
   and finely chopped
sea salt (optional)
sunflower oil, to fry in

To serve
smoked oil
3 tablespoons mayonnaise
smoked paprika

1 Stir a little smoked oil through the mayonnaise and set aside.

2 Mix all the ingredients, except the beetroot and oil, together in a mixing bowl and stir until smooth, firm and well combined. Add the beetroot and stir gently into the mixture so it doesn't stain the mince red. The mixture might need a little salt, but the capers are salty so don't overdo it. At this point, you can fry a small amount of the mixture to test the saltiness, then add more if needed. Shape the mixture into about 36 smooth meatballs, each about 30g and the size of a table tennis ball.

3 Heat a thin layer of oil that just covers the surface of a large frying pan over a medium-high heat. It is important that the pan and the oil are both hot before adding the meatballs, because the meatballs will fall apart if the oil isn't hot enough. Add as many balls as will fit, without overcrowding, and fry the meatballs for about 3 minutes until they are browned and crispy. I prefer these when they are raw in the middle, which is why they are only fried for just a few minutes – the point is to colour them, not cook them. Pan-fry in batches, if necessary, and serve as soon as they are cooked, so everyone gets a couple helpings of freshly fried meatballs.

4 These balls can be served directly from the frying pan on the table; they should be hot outside and still rare in the middle. Alternatively, arrange the meatballs on plates and top with a little smoked mayonnaise and sprinkle with paprika.

Galician-style Cod Balls

I served these to my friends in a rich white wine sauce, with caviar for extra luxury, but the Tomatoes in Dill Cream (page 64) go very well too. And, if you want to take the Spanish theme further, add a plate of grilled padrón peppers sprinkled with grated Manchego on the side.

Makes about 32 balls

700g cod fillets, skinned and
   minced
1 tablespoon sea salt
200ml whipping cream
20g bottarga (dried fish roe),
   finely grated
dried seaweed, such as wakame
   (you need about 50g per litre
   of water)
100g black caviar, to serve

For the white wine sauce

100g butter, chopped
2 shallots, finely chopped
1 bottle (750ml) good Chablis
500ml whipping cream
sea salt and freshly ground
   white pepper

1 Beat the cod with the salt until the mince becomes firmer. Stir in the cream and bottarga and continue beating until smooth, firm and well combined. Cover and transfer to the fridge for 1 hour to chill.

2 With dampened hands, shape the mixture into about 32 smooth balls, 30g each and the size of a table tennis ball. Return the cod balls to the fridge for another hour.

3 Meanwhile, bring a large pan of water to a simmer, then make the white wine sauce. For the sauce, melt the butter in a large, heavy-based saucepan over a low heat. Add the shallots and fry, stirring occasionally, for about 10 minutes until softened but not coloured. Add the wine and bring to the boil, scraping the bottom of the pan. Reduce the heat and simmer, uncovered, for about 30 minutes until reduced by half. Add the cream and continue simmering over a medium heat for 5 minutes. Use a stick blender to purée the sauce – the shallots will give it a bit of body. Season with salt and pepper and keep hot while you cook the cod balls.

4 To cook the cod balls, add the dried seaweed to the pan of simmering water. Carefully add as many cod balls as will fit to the pan, without overcrowding, and simmer until they float to the surface and are cooked through when you cut one open; if they aren't cooked through, simmer for a further 2 minutes and test again. It is important that they do not boil, as they are prone to cracking. Using a slotted spoon, remove the cod balls from the water and drain on kitchen paper.

5 Reheat the sauce, if necessary. Spoon it on to a warmed serving platter, add the cod balls and garnish with black caviar. The fish balls should be creamy and taste of the sea from both the dried fish roe and the seaweed.

Ch. 6   Family Lunch

Eating a family lunch together is something we should all do more often. I love it when my children spend time with their grandmother, aunt and cousins, while I'm busy in the kitchen making the best food I know.

For this menu I have taken inspiration from one of my favourite countries, Greece. I have visited many times and always long to return when winter is coming to an end. The meatballs I served for my family feast showcased the sunny flavours of the Aegean with olives, feta cheese and oregano. I then rounded out the Mediterranean theme with a typical Greek Salad (page 108), crisp Rice Balls (page 109), large platters of chargrilled vegetables and slabs of olive-oil-drizzled feta cheese with orange wedges for squeezing over. If you can't be sitting at a seaside taverna, I think this is as good as it gets.

A Greek-inspired Family Lunch

 These Greek meatballs are regularly on the menu at Meatballs for the People and are very popular with adults and children, so they are a natural choice for a family meal. Here I serve them with garlic- and rosemary-infused crushed potatoes for something a little different.

Serves 6 (generously); makes about 62 balls

400g veal mince, with the highest fat content you can buy
300g lamb mince
300g pork mince
2 eggs
50g pitted green olives, finely chopped
1 tablespoon dried oregano
1 tablespoon shredded parsley
200g feta cheese, coarsely crumbled
sunflower oil, for frying
sea salt and freshly ground black pepper

For the tzatziki

500g full-fat, strained Greek yogurt
50ml virgin olive oil, plus extra for serving
½ cucumber, halved, peeled, deseeded and thinly sliced
1 tablespoon lemon juice
1 tablespoon finely shredded fresh mint

1 You can prepare the tzatziki up to 3 days in advance; the longer it is stored the more intense the garlic taste will become. Mix all the ingredients, except the garlic, with salt to taste and stir well. Stir in half the garlic and taste; personally, I like it with lots of garlic so I usually add it all, but it's totally up to you. Transfer to a serving bowl, cover and set aside in the fridge until ready to serve.

2 Bring a large saucepan of salted water to the boil for the potatoes.

3 To prepare the meatballs, beat the veal, lamb and pork minces with the eggs in a large mixing bowl, using a wooden spoon, until the mixture becomes firmer. Beat in the olives, oregano and parsley until smooth and well blended. Add the feta cheese then give it a very light mix to avoid breaking up the feta too much; you want some larger pieces throughout the mixture. If the mince is too firm, you can add a little water to loosen. Shape the mixture into about 62 smooth meatballs, each 30g and the size of a table tennis ball. Set aside in the fridge while you make the potatoes.

4 Add the potatoes to the boiling salted water and boil for about 20 minutes until tender, then drain well.

5 While the potatoes are boiling, preheat the oven to 230°C/Fan 210°C/Gas 8.

6 After the potatoes are drained, transfer them to an ovenproof serving dish large enough to hold them in a single layer. Use a potato masher to flatten the potatoes; they should be crushed, but not completely smooth. Spoon over the olive oil, then transfer the dish to the oven and roast the potatoes

4 teaspoons ouzo
2 garlic cloves, or to taste,
   crushed

For the crushed potatoes
1kg unpeeled potatoes – my
   favourites are new potatoes
   in season
180ml olive oil
4 garlic cloves, unpeeled and left
   whole, bashed
needles from 1 large sprig
   rosemary

To serve
Greek Salad (page 108)
Rice Balls (page 109)
feta cheese with orange wedges
platters of chargrilled vegetables,
   drizzled with extra-virgin
   olive oil

for about 20 minutes. The potatoes are already cooked, so now you're just getting them a little crispy. When they begin to crisp, add the garlic cloves and roast for a further 5 minutes. Throw in the rosemary and roast for another 1–2 minutes. Just before serving, stir the garlic and rosemary through the potatoes and sprinkle with salt. Keep hot until ready to serve.

7   Meanwhile, fry the meatballs. Melt enough sunflower oil in a large frying pan over a medium heat to come about one-third of the way up the meatballs. Add as many meatballs as will fit, without overcrowding, and fry, turning frequently, for 10–15 minutes until brown on the outside and cooked through when you cut one open. Pan-fry in batches, if necessary. As each batch is fried use a slotted spoon to transfer it to a baking tray and keep hot. Finish by sprinkling with a little salt and a couple of turns of the peppermill.

8   When you're ready to serve, stir in any liquid that has accumulated on top of the tzatziki, then drizzle over some olive oil. Serve alongside the meatballs and crushed potatoes, with a Greek Salad and Rice Balls.

Greek Salad

 Good food is guaranteed to spark certain memories for me and a fresh Greek salad is close to my heart after the special holidays we've enjoyed there. Wherever you find a Greek family, you'll find some great feta cheese and hardy olives nearby.

Serves 6

400g watermelon, rinded and
cut into cubes
6 tomatoes in a variety of
colours, cut into wedges
2 green peppers, cored and
roughly chopped
1 large red onion, roughly sliced
1 stalk pale celery, sliced
½ cucumber, roughly chopped
2 tablespoons fresh oregano
leaves
1 tablespoon shredded mint
1 tablespoon shredded flat-leaf
parsley
200ml virgin olive oil
100ml red wine vinegar
400g feta cheese, crumbled
200g green olives

1   Mix the vegetables and herbs in a large bowl. Whisk together the olive oil and vinegar in a separate bowl or jug, then pour over the salad. Give everything a good stir to mix then top with the crumbled feta and olives.

Rice Balls

 These little morsels are inspired by Italian arancini. They can be tricky to make, but are well worth the effort.

Makes about 24 balls, serves 6

about 1.2 litres water
280g arborio rice
200g feta cheese
about 60g panko breadcrumbs
vegetable oil, for deep frying

1 Pour the water into a saucepan and bring to the boil, then reduce the heat and keep at a simmer. Put the rice in a separate pan, add a ladleful of the water and bring to the boil. Reduce the heat to low and simmer, stirring frequently, until the liquid has been absorbed by the rice, then stir in another ladleful of simmering water. Repeat this gradual addition of water and stirring for about 25 minutes until the rice is tender. You want the rice to be creamy and almost overcooked. Transfer to a large bowl and leave to cool at room temperature.

2 When the rice is cold, crumble in the feta cheese and beat together until combined. Shape the mixture into about 24 balls, 40g each and the size of a golf ball. It is important that the balls are well compacted, otherwise they will fall apart during cooking. Roll the balls in a thin layer of breadcrumbs so they are coated all over.

3 Heat enough oil for deep-frying in a deep-fat fryer or heavy-based pan to 180°C on a digital thermometer. (If you don't have a digital thermometer, the oil is ready when a small piece of the mixture sizzles and rises to the surface straightaway when dropped into the hot oil.) Deep-fry for about 4 minutes until golden brown. Fry in batches to avoid over-crowding the pan, checking the temperature after each batch. As each batch is fried, use a slotted spoon to transfer it to an ovenproof platter lined with greaseproof or kitchen paper to drain and keep hot. These are best served straightaway.

Ch. 7   Our Best Sides

1-2-3 Ättika Pickling Liquid

Historically, we Swedes pickled to preserve food for the winter months, but now we do it mostly for the taste – and, of course, the long shelf-life is a bonus. In the modern Scandinavian cuisine that has recently taken the world by storm, pickling has a natural place as a taste maker.

The secret behind most things that are pickled in Swedish cuisine is ättika – a type of strong white vinegar. You should be able to source it online, but if you do not have access to ättika, buy the strongest white vinegar you can find. It will not be the same, but it should be okay. The version we use at Meatballs for the People has a strength of 12% or 24% acetic acid.

This recipe is the foundation of everything we pickle in the restaurant. It is also one of the world's easiest recipes.

1 part ättika, 12% or 24%
2 parts sugar
3 parts water

1   Mix all ingredients until the sugar dissolves, and it's ready to use. Store indefinitely in a sterilised, glass jar with a vinegar-proof lid.

Classic Lingonberries

This is a traditional recipe I flavour with cinnamon.

Serves 10–12

500g lingonberries, fresh or
    frozen
200g granulated sugar
8cm piece cinnamon stick

1   Mix the lingonberries and sugar in a mixing bowl, gently mashing about one-third of the berries. Leave to stand until the sugar dissolves, then add the cinnamon stick to flavour.

2   Transfer into a sterilised glass jar with an airtight lid and leave to infuse in the fridge for at least 3 hours. These can be stored in the fridge for up to 3 months in a sealed jar.

Grandpa's Lingonberries

This is an original family recipe, flavoured with one of my favourite tipples, whisky. It makes for a lovely gift for family and friends.

Serves 10–12

500g lingonberries, fresh or frozen
200g granulated sugar
1 nice splash of good smokey whisky – or to taste

1　Mix the lingonberries, sugar and whisky in a mixing bowl, gently mashing about one-third of the berries. Leave to stand until the sugar dissolves, then add some more whisky, if desired.

2　Transfer the lingonberries and any liquid into a beautiful, sterilised glass jar with an airtight lid. Leave to infuse in the fridge for at least 3 hours, and serve at the table along with your meatballs. Anything leftover will keep in the fridge for up to 3 months in the sealed jar.

Finger Cucumber

with a hint of kimchi

This cucumber pickle can be eaten at room temperature or cold, and is also great with a little chopped fresh coriander added just before serving.

Serves 10

500g cucumber, cut into chunks
500ml 1-2-3 Ättika Pickling
   Liquid (page 112)
100ml pickling liquid from your
   favourite kimchi

1 Mix all the ingredients in a sterilised glass jar with an air-tight, vinegar-proof lid and seal. Transfer to the fridge for a couple of days before using, shaking the jar gently a couple of times. It continues to change character over time as the fermentation continues, so it will get stronger. It will keep in the sealed jar in the fridge for up to 4 weeks.

Summer Cucumber

with crown dill

For me, cucumber is the melon of vegetables; it is mild tasting with a lot of freshness, perfect to flavour in different ways, and is great in a gin and tonic, too.

Serves 10

500ml water
200ml white wine vinegar
2 tablespoons sea salt
1 tablespoon sugar
500g cucumber with a thick skin, sliced with a vegetable crinkle cutter
10 crown dill sprigs, or fresh dill sprigs

1 At least 2 weeks before planning to serve, bring the water, vinegar, salt and sugar to the boil, stirring to dissolve the salt and sugar, and boil for 2 minutes. Turn off the heat and leave to cool completely in the pan.

2 Layer the cucumber and crown dill sprigs in a sterilised glass jar with an air-tight and vinegar-proof lid. Pour over the brine to cover, seal and keep in the fridge to mature for at least 2 weeks before using. Any leftovers can be stored in the sealed jar in the fridge for up to 4 weeks. Just before serving, I refresh the crown dill sprigs with fresh ones.

Sweet Parsley Cucumber

This cucumber is the most popular pickle at Meatballs for the People.
We serve it with virtually everything on the menu.

Serves 10

500g cucumber, scrubbed and
  very thinly sliced
300ml 1-2-3 Ättika Pickling
  Liquid (page 112)
50g curly parsley, finely chopped

1 Mix all the ingredients in a non-metallic bowl and leave to marinate for
  about 2 hours. Enjoy! Any leftover cucumber can be kept in the covered
  bowl in the fridge for up to 2 days, but this is a pickle I like to serve soon
  after making.

Cauliflower Pickles

in pink gin

Pickled cauliflower is even tastier, if that's even possible, when swimming in pink gin and rose petals. This is a beautiful dish and a really luxurious variation on everyday pickles.

Serves 4–6

1 medium head cauliflower,
   divided into florets
1 litre 1-2-3 Ättika Pickling Liquid
   (page 112)
200ml of your favourite pink gin
petals from 3 edible roses

1 Bring the cauliflower and Ättika Pickling Liquid to the boil in a saucepan, then boil for about 7 minutes until the florets are soft, but still retaining some bite. Remove the saucepan from the heat and leave the florets cool in the liquid, then stir in the pink gin followed by the rose petals. It's ready to use, so serve in a nice glass bowl. If not serving immediately, store in a sterilised container with an air-tight and vinegar-proof lid in the fridge for up to 4 weeks, but don't stir in the rose petals until just before serving.

Colourful Carrots

with mustard seeds

There are few things as good as a carrot just pulled straight from the earth – you can't beat fresh produce. And, of course, you can make this with everyday orange carrots, but why not have a bit of fun when the multi-coloured variety?

Serves 4–6

500g carrots, preferably different
   colours and varieties, peeled
   and cut into beautiful shapes
1 litre 1-2-3 Ättika Pickling Liquid
   (page 112)
10 black peppercorns, crushed
5 fresh bay leaves
2 tablespoons white mustard
   seeds

1   Bring the carrots, Ättika Pickling Liquid, peppercorns, bay leaves and mustard seeds to the boil in a saucepan and boil for about 10 minutes, or until the carrots are soft, depending on their size. Turn off the heat and leave the carrots to cool in the liquid in the saucepan.

2   Use a slotted spoon to transfer the carrots to a bowl and serve straightaway. Any leftovers can be stored in a sterilised glass jar with an air-tight and vinegar-proof lid in the fridge for up to 4 weeks.

Sweet-and-Spicy Green Tomatoes

I learnt this recipe as a young chef in the 1990s, when we served it as an accompaniment to venison, and now it's a favourite on our menus.

Serves 4–6

1 litre 1-2-3 Ättika Pickling Liquid (page 112)
5 star anise
8cm piece cinnamon stick
1 tablespoon green cardamom pods, lightly crushed
500g green tomatoes, cut into wedges

1   At least a day before you want to serve these, bring the Ättika Pickling Liquid to the boil in a saucepan with the star anise and cinnamon stick. Turn off the heat, add the tomatoes and leave the liquid to cool. Transfer the tomatoes and liquid to a sterilised glass jar with an air-tight and vinegar-proof lid and leave for at least 1 day before using. These will last for up to 4 weeks in the sealed jar in the fridge.

Tangy Rhubarb
with ginger and fennel seeds

There is nothing like the taste of rhubarb, and as a child I was lucky enough to eat rhubarb all summer, directly from the land. As a chef, I like to use rhubarb in my food as soon as it is season, however, in Sweden, much like an avocado, a perfectly ripe rhubarb is difficult to find: not ripe, not ripe, then it is suddenly overripe! This is particularly good early in the season, when rhubarb is tender and pink, and not too tough.

When you boil it, cook it so that it still has some resistance but is cooked through. My top tip is to make sure that your rhubarb is cut to evenly-sized pieces so it will all be done at the same time and none of it will be overcooked.

Serves 10

1 litre 1-2-3 Ättika Pickling Liquid (page 112)
500g rhubarb, peeled, with the peel reserved and the stalks cut into even lengths
50g sushi ginger
1 tablespoon fennel seeds

1 Bring the Ättika Pickling Liquid and rhubarb peel to the boil in a saucepan, then reduce the heat to medium and simmer for 5 minutes, or until the liquid has a beautiful pink colour. Strain and discard the peel, then return the liquid to the saucepan.

2 Add the rhubarb pieces, sushi ginger and fennel seeds. Return the liquid to the boil, then reduce the heat and simmer for 1 minute. Turn off the heat and leave to cool in the pan. Transfer to sterilised glass jars with air-tight and vinegar-proof lids, and leave to infuse in the fridge for 1–2 days until it's ready to use. This will keep in a sealed jar in the fridge for up to 4 weeks.

Hasselback Potatoes

This is my variation of traditional hasselback potatoes. For me, the perfectly cooked potato is crisp on the outside, while still fluffy on the inside – just like a classic fondant potato – and here, I've made it even more special with the flavour of lots of butter, extra crispiness from breadcrumbs and seasoned with bay leaves.

These are delicious with so many of the recipes in the book, but especially Grandma's Meatballs (page 48), North African-style Lamb Balls (page 80) or The Rooster and the Lobster (page 83).

Makes 12

250g butter, melted
12 medium floury potatoes,
  about 70g each, peeled
12 fresh bay leaves, halved
80g dried breadcrumbs
sea salt

1 Preheat the oven to 200°C/Fan 180°C/Gas 6, and grease a roasting tin large enough to hold the potatoes in a single layer with a little of the melted butter.

2 Using a thin, sharp knife, carefully slice all along the width of each potato at 0.5cm intervals without cutting all the way through. The best way to do this is by putting the handle of a chopstick or thin wooden spoon on either side of the potato and then cutting straight down; the piece of wood stops you from cutting right through. Slide 2 halves of a bay leaf between the slices of each potato.

3 Place the potatoes in the tin and pour the remaining melted butter over them, making sure it goes between all the slices, then generously sprinkle with salt. Roast in the oven for about 45 minutes, basting with the butter every 15 minutes, again making sure it goes between the slices, until the potatoes are tender and beginning to turn golden.

4 Increase the oven temperature to 220°C/Fan 200°C/Gas 7. Baste the potatoes one last time and sprinkle with the breadcrumbs. Continue roasting them for a further 15 minutes, or until they are a beautiful golden colour and take on the shape of accordions. They are ready to serve.

Cranberry Ketchup

This spicy condiment is served with everything at Meatballs for the People. Use as large or as small a piece of chipotle chilli as you like, depending on how spicy you like your food.

Makes about 500g

500g cranberries, thawed if frozen
300ml 1-2-3 Ättika Pickle (page 112)
1 piece dried chipotle chilli
1 teaspoon ground allspice

1 Put all the ingredients in a food processor, and purée until smooth. Transfer to a heavy-based saucepan over a medium heat and simmer, stirring, until thickened. It will become thicker as it cools, so if it's looking too thick, stir in a little water.

2 Pour the hot ketchup into warmed, sterilised bottles with air-tight and vinegar-proof lids. Use within 3 months. Once opened, store in the fridge. Alternatively, leave to cool and store in the fridge in squeezy bottles for up to 3 weeks.

Apple and Horseradish Compôte

Apple and horseradish are a perfect pairing. As a young chef I learned to make a variation of this compôte for a classic dish from the Alps, *tafelspitz*. The compôte has been around ever since and it feels great that it gets to be among all the meatballs.

Serves 4–6

5 apples, peeled, cored and finely chopped
3 tablespoons lemon juice
50g granulated sugar
4 teaspoons very finely chopped curly parsley
100g fresh horseradish, peeled and grated

1   Put half the apples and all the lemon juice in a saucepan over a low heat, stirring and beating with a wooden spoon until the apples are soft and mushy. Add the remaining apple pieces and the sugar and cook for about 5 minutes, stirring frequently, until the apples are soft, but not falling apart. You want to retain some texture in the compôte. Remove the pan from the heat and leave the mixture to cool completely.

2   Stir in the parsley and most of the horseradish. Transfer to a serving bowl and sprinkle over the remaining horseradish to serve. If not serving immediately, cover and chill in the fridge for up to 3 days. Return to room temperature and sprinkle with the extra horseradish just before serving.

Ch. 8   Index

About the Author

Mathias Pilbad was born in Stockholm. From an early age he had a love of food and cooking for others, so a career in catering was a natural fit. He soon started as an apprentice, getting some classical training before moving on to work in some of Stockholm's best, award-winning restaurants throughout his career, learning something new at each one. In 2000 he competed with the Swedish Culinary Olympics team, winning a gold medal.

In 2003, Mathias took the plunge and set up his first restaurant with two friends on one of Stockholm's beautiful archipelagos, and has since opened a number of other restaurants. In 2013 Meatballs for the People was born, quickly becoming a mecca for tourists and travellers from around the world, as well as much-loved restaurant for locals.

Publisher
Jon Croft

Commissioning Editor
Meg Boas

Senior Editor
Emily North

Designer
Anika Schulze

Photography Art Director
Peter Moffat

Photographers
Andreas Sjöstrand and
Fredrik Bohman

Copyeditor
Beverly LeBlanc

Home Economist
Susanna Tee

Proofreader
Susan Low

Indexer
Zoe Ross